Analysis and
Value Judgment

Analysis and Value Judgment

Carl Dahlhaus

Translated from the German by Siegmund Levarie

Monographs in Musicology No. 1

PENDRAGON PRESS
NEW YORK

Forthcoming Titles in the **MONOGRAPHS IN MUSICOLOGY SERIES**

No. 2 LA STATIRA *by Pietro Ottoboni and Alessandro Scarlatti:*
The Textual Sources, with a Documentary Postscript by
Willian C. Holmes (1983)

No. 3 *Arts, Sciences, Alloys* by Iannis Xenakis (in press)

No. 4 *Alessandro Scarlatti's* Gli equivoci nel sembiante: *The*
History of a Baroque Opera by Frank D'Accone (in press)

Library of Congress Cataloging in Publication Data

Dahlhaus, Carl, 1928-
   Analysis and value judgement.

   (Pendragon Press monographs in musicology
series ; 1)
   Translation of: Analyse un Werturteil.
   1. Music-- Analysis, appreciation. 2. Music --
Philosophy and aesthetics. I. Title. II. Series.
MT6.D128A53 1982   780'.1   82-12251
ISBN 0-918728-20-7

Originally published in 1970 as *Analyse und Werturteil*
   from the series *Musikpädagogik, Forschung und*
   Lehre, Volume 8.

By permission of B. SCHOTT'S SÖHNE
           Music Publishers
           Mainz, W. Germany

Contents

v

Analyses 57

Preface

The attempt to prove aesthetic judgments by a critique of musical forms may appear hybrid; the opinion that value judgments are nothing but open or masked judgments of taste—admitting argument but no conclusion to the argument—is just as firmly rooted as the complementary conviction that musical analysis is "free of value judgment." (Whoever claims or postulates the separation of analysis and aesthetic judgment may either complain about the inadequacy of analysis which eschews conclusiveness or praise the scientific character of analysis as demonstrated by asceticism toward value judgments.)

On the other hand, one cannot deny the insistent thought of a possible reconciliation between analysis and aesthetic judgment; one cannot easily dispose of it as a bad utopia. We need hardly say that the attempt must remain fragmentary and that it breaks off again and again instead of reaching a conclusion. The aesthetic reflections upon premises and criteria of musical judgment aim less at the solution than at the definition of problems. And the analyses, while neglecting melody and texture, restrict themselves to a critique of musical forms and thus are one-sided. (Yet the author does not wish to escape criticism by feigning unpretentiousness: the mere choice of his theme proves the opposite.)

We need not justify at length this investigation of analysis and value judgment. Analysis of individual musical works is indispensable in music instruction (understood as artistic instruction), which does not yet possess firm aesthetic dogmas that could render superfluous the study of specific and unique cases. However, precisely because dogmas have become fragile, the question of proving a musical value judgment arises in almost every classroom. While the method of technical and formal analysis has established itself, the problem of entanglement in value judgments has become ever more difficult and pressing. The one development appears as the reverse of the other: both insight into the necessity of analyzing the particularity of an individual case (and not as a mere example of a generality) and feelings of doubt concerning value judgments are consequences of the disintegration of classical dogmatism, which dominated nineteenth-century aesthetic and pedagogic musical thought. An aesthetic judgment, however, not founded on a norm can proceed only from the recognition of the particularity of an individual work, that is, from an analysis.

PREMISES

Value judgment and objective judgment

To consider aesthetic judgments "subjective" and nothing else is a cliché whose meaning is vague and indefinite but whose function is unambiguous: it serves the purpose of rendering reflection and rational justification unnecessary. The cliché thus belongs, in the words of Francis Bacon, to the idols of indolence. Whoever refers to it feels justified in insisting on his own judgment without letting himself be diverted by arguments which might imperil the premises of the judgment. Individual particular taste, which in general is not at all individual but rather a reflex of group norms, appears as the highest authority against which there is no appeal.

Arguments based on objective facts become suspect as offering not a foundation but merely an illustration of aesthetic judgment, which passes for one of feeling. Rationality appears as a secondary factor, as an addition or decoration. Skepticism, however, which fancies itself sovereign is rather empty. Distrust itself deserves distrust.

First, one must distinguish the origin, the genesis, of an aesthetic judgment from its legitimation. There is no denying that subjective judgment provides the psychological premise and point of departure for the discovery of rational explanations; but this does not exclude that reason, not subjective reaction, decides whether the judgment is valid or not.

3

Second, subjective judgments about music, at least relevant ones, contain earlier musical experiences and insights that do not necessarily become explicitly conscious. Thus, in fortunate cases, proof and rational foundation are not an external appendix or a pseudo-logical disguise of the irrational but a discovery of what always underlay subjective judgment albeit tacitly. The attempt to justify one's first impression is at the same time a return to its premises.

Third, in one's resistance to accepting arguments seriously with the risk of having to disavow one's first vague judgment lives an aristocratic, anti-bourgeois attitude. Obtuse opposition to rationality is not a natural quality but a historical mark of aesthetic judgment. In the seventeenth and eighteenth centuries, the concept of taste, as with Gracian and Dubos, was an aristocratic category: taste was a social privilege which one did not promote rationally but asserted irrationally. (The origin and history of the concept explain the sensitivity against reproach of bad taste—the strange fact that aesthetic verdicts seem harder to bear than moral: the aesthetic reproach indicates an offense against social self-respect and ambition.) Inasmuch as suspicion of rationality in aesthetics is an aristocratic or pseudo-aristocratic relic—a piece of the past in the thought of the present—it need not be accepted as if it were objectively founded; it can be suspended or even turned into its opposite: suspicion of aesthetic irrationality. In any case, there is no cause for submitting to the arrogant prejudice which considers arguments as unnecessary pedantry of which anyone claiming good taste ought to feel ashamed.

While the conviction of mere "subjectivity" in aesthetic judgment is thus motivated by laziness and arrogance, the formulation of the idea of "objectivity" is nevertheless difficult if one wishes to do justice to the premises of aesthetic judgments.

1. The psychological postulate that one must approach an issue with rigorous self-denial in order to be objective, instead of becoming enmeshed in feelings, seems to be trivial. But it is questionable to the extent that judgments based on feelings form the starting point for the discovery of rational causes of judgment; they are not the highest but rather the first authority. Objectivity arises, not from the critic's forgetting and extinguishing himself, but

rather from the effort to mediate between the aesthetic object and inherent attributes of the subject. Just as a judgment based on feelings without objective content is empty, so too is any attempt at objectivity without the substance supplied by emotion.

2. There is validity to the sociological identification of "objectivity" with "intersubjectivity"—mutual agreement of the subjects—as long as common sense, normal perception, and "general and prevalent reason" suffice to judge a given case sensibly. Ambivalence enters when a judgment, in order to be adequate, demands premises that are nearly inaccessible and rare: "intersubjectivity of the initiated" is almost a contradiction in itself. Common sense in music is the "natural musical feeling," which became the aesthetic authority in the eighteenth century, the epoch of philanthropism, and of which the decisive criteria are the "appearance of familiarity" and expressiveness within the limits of beauty. While it would be unjust simply to indict musical common sense as blinkered, one cannot deny that it has been at odds with the development of music—a development concerned less with the "appearance of familiarity" than with the abruptly new. "Objectivity" as "intersubjectivity" is thus an authority whose importance and legitimacy are subject to historical changes.

3. "Objectivity" is not a quality, either given or not given, but a postulate more or less complied with. And one must not expect of an aesthetic judgment a degree of "objectivity" unattained even by a musically factual judgment. Whoever presumes a rigorous concept of objectivity and demands that a musical phenomenon, to be objectively valid, must have a cause grounded in the acoustical structure could deny the objective existence of strong beats in a measure; instead of deriving always from the same acoustical basis, they are marked by changing and divergent means—not only by dynamic accents but also by small agogic expansions or by regularly recurring rhythmic or harmonic patterns. Strong beats in a measure are, in phenomenological terms, not "real" but "intentionally" given; yet they are "objective"—characteristics of the object. Also "objective" are the emotional qualities attached to musical works. The expression of mourning is experienced as a quality of the "music itself," not as a condition of the subject; recognizing funeral music, we neither necessarily draw any

conclusion concerning the emotions of the composer or interpreter, nor need we be sad ourselves. In musical experience, objectivity thus exists in shades and gradations. A pitch depending on frequency, a strong beat in a measure of which the acoustical substratum is interchangeable, an emotional character which appears as a quality of the music itself without being a "real" attribute, and finally an aesthetic judgment ascribing to a work "greatness" or "perfection"—all these denote different degrees of objectivity. And whereas an aesthetic judgment is undeniably less objective than the determination of a pitch, it yet has a right to claim objectivity. Every judgment, as soon as it is pronounced, implies this claim.

4. In order to be tenable, value judgments, including the apparently harmless "subjective" ones, must be supported by factual judgments at least roughly adequate to the case. Anyone missing expressive melodies in a sonata form built on the principle of thematic-motivic development and therefore condemning the work aesthetically articulates not an unarguable taste but rather passes an incorrect judgment rendered irrelevant by the misinterpretation of the sonata form as a miscarried potpourri.

However, when aesthetic judgment depends on an underlying factual judgment, the positivist thesis, according to which aesthetic judgments are founded on nothing else but "group norms" beyond the cogency of personal decision, becomes invalid. Positivism restricted to collecting opinions is not positivistic enough because it does not involve itself with the matter itself, the musical works. It is an error to grant to a "group norm" which considers a pop tune the essence of music and a Beethoven symphony a hollow din equal aesthetic privileges as to the opposite "group norm." The factual judgments underlying the "group norms" are not equally founded. A listener capable of doing justice to a Beethoven symphony is generally equipped to cope with the musical issues of a pop tune, but the reverse is not true. Arrogance of the initiated must not be defended, but that nobody has the right to blame musical illiterates for being illiterate does not change the fact that illiteracy provides a weak foundation for aesthetic judgments.

Aesthetics, analysis, theory

Aesthetic judgments, at least the cogent ones, are sustained by factual judgments which in turn depend on analytic methods demonstrating the musical attitude of a period. And inversely, analytic procedures, including those without preconceptions, are tied to aesthetic premises.

A paradigm for the connection of analysis and aesthetics is the theory of sonata form around 1800. In the late eighteenth century, in Heinrich Christoph Koch's treatise on composition based on works by Haydn, sonata form was conceived in principle as a monothematic form. The second subject passed for an incidental thought and not for a contrast to the main theme; the concept of thematic dialectics was foreign to Koch. Unmistakable is the dependence of the theory of forms on aesthetics, the influence of the dogma of the unity of affect that must rule in one movement—a unity which tolerates deviations but never contrasts. The analytic method of defining contrasts as modifications and an aesthetics viewing unity of affect as a condition for the inner cohesion of a musical piece support each other mutually.

No less dependent on aesthetic premises than Koch's method is the opposite procedure developed by Adolf Bernhard Marx half a century later, which draws out contrasts and conceives them as constituents of musical form. Marx, who recognized thematic dualism as the main principle of sonata form, was a Hegelian (in North Germany in the 1830s it was difficult not to be one); he oriented himself by the philosophic model of Hegelian dialectics in order to give an aesthetic foundation to the theory of musical forms, particularly the theory of sonata form, the then prevailing formal type. One cannot deny that, apart from the difference in aesthetic premises, the historic development of the musical form itself—the far-reaching modification of sonata form by Beethoven—suggested or forced a change of theory. The relevance of aesthetic dogmas, however, manifests itself negatively in the tendency toward distortions of musical facts by every analytic method: whereas Koch tried to reduce thematic contrasts to mere modifications, Marx followed the opposite tendency of exaggerating deviations or episodes as contrasts.

Although analysis thus depends on the aesthetics that determine the musical thought of an epoch, it remains in close reciprocal relation with theory, that is, the systems of harmony, rhythm, and form. A piece of theory, explicitly or tacitly, provides the starting point for each analysis. The notion of a description without assumptions is a phantom; if it could be realized, it would not be worth the trouble. Inversely, analyses of musical works are what supplies the foundation of a theory not rooted in thin air. Theory can be both the precondition and also the goal and result of musical analyses. Thus an attempt to define more precisely the concept of musical analysis may justifiably proceed from the relation of analysis to theory.

1. Theory based on analyses which it employs merely as means originates through abstraction; the single case, the object of the analysis, appears as an interchangeable example of a rule. On the other hand, an analysis individualizes which implies theoretic thoughts without aiming at a theoretic system. It attempts to do justice to the particular and unrepeatable; the general, the theory, is but a means and instrument for the attempt to understand the unique individual case. This effort exhausts itself in approximations but nevertheless deserves to be stubbornly repeated.

A model of a procedure combining theory and analysis is the reductive method of Heinrich Schenker, his "doctrine of layers." The reduction to the same *Ursatz* of works with completely dissimilar foregrounds certainly pertains to theory—theory of rigorous character. The procedure abstracts. The analyses appear as means to support the hypothesis that significant musical works within the tradition from Bach to Brahms always are structured on an *Ursatz*.

This theory, on the other hand, may become an instrument for analysis. The description of a single work may thus be understood as a kind of genetic representation, as an attempt to reconstruct the work "from the inside out:" from the *Ursatz* through "prolongations," various "layers" of the work arise to the foreground transmitted by the notated text.

Schenker interlaces theory and analysis with aesthetic judgments. Works admired as "masterworks" by Schenker, who was a musical conservative, must contain an *Ursatz:* the theory of the

Ursatz is in fact nothing else but the foundation of musical premises for the greatness of the "masterworks." The tradition which distinguishes a work as "masterly" is measured by the theory of the *Ursatz*, and inversely the theory is measured by the tradition. (If an unquestionable "masterwork" lacked the *Ursatz*, the theory, according to Schenker's own criteria, would be endangered.) If, however, as in works by Reger and Stravinsky, no *Ursatz* is to be found notwithstanding persistent analytic efforts, then Schenker does not hesitate to issue an aesthetic verdict.

2. Musical analysis, to put it banally, is either a means or an end. It aims at theory and is thus its first step; or it tries to do justice to a musical work as a particular individual formation. The distinction between theoretically and aesthetically oriented analyses may appear pedantic but is not superfluous. All too often, musical analyses or analytic fragments, most of all descriptions of harmonies and tonality, suffer from turbidity of purpose and hence provoke the suspicion that they are useless. Analyses deserving this title are, on the one hand, efforts to demonstrate the validity of a theory, of the system of functions and scale degrees; the possibility of a consistent and through its simplicity persuasive designation of chords by functional symbols or degree numbers then serves as proof; it reveals less about the work than about the theory. Or, on the other hand, an analysis should isolate the characteristics that distinguish the harmonic structure of one work from that of another. In this case it does not suffice to number the chords and to let the reader find in these numbers the special quality of the harmonic structure. The individual character of the chord structures and relations must rather be expressly shown and articulated by an interpretation of the analysis: an analysis of a second order (of which the categories have hardly been developed). If—so one may conclude—an analysis functions neither as demonstration or proof of a theory nor as a conceptual transcription of the particularity of a work, then it is unnecessary: it appears as mere application of a nomenclature, as labeling, which says nothing because it is aimless.

3. Theoretically oriented analysis treats a piece of music as a document, as testimonial for facts outside itself or for a rule transcending the single case. Aesthetically oriented analysis, on the other

hand, understands the same piece as a work complete in itself and existing for its own sake. To this difference between document and work corresponds, at least roughly, a difference between partial and comprehensive analysis. Without losing significance and validity, a theory may deal with only a part of the music, with harmony or rhythm; it even must do so in order to avoid getting lost in an endless muddle. An analysis, however, which conceives a piece as a work always addresses, at least by intention, the work as a whole. The object of analysis which proceeds by individualizing is not harmony by itself but rather harmony in connection with rhythm and musical syntax. Only when the interlacing network of the various moments of the composition has been rendered clear and intelligible will there emerge the particularity and individual character of a work, escaping one-sided analysis restricted to harmony or rhythm.

4. Musical rhythm and first of all harmony form the object of theories in the strict sense of the word, whereas systems of melody and form tend to dissolve themselves in analyses of separate works. This divergence is as obvious as it is puzzling. A theory of musical forms which proceeds by generalizations and abstractions invites the suspicion of forcible schematization which distorts the facts; the theory of harmony actually tends no less toward schematization without, however, being reproached for it. And the feeling or prejudice that harmony is more amenable to theory, and form more to analysis, has had a far-reaching influence on the development of analytic methods. As rudimentary as they still appear, the categories of form analysis are sufficiently differentiated to make possible the description of an individual form. Efforts, on the other hand, to establish a harmonic analysis capable of a comparable approximation to the musically particular are negligible; and this shortcoming, severe as it is, is not even felt as one.

Functional, aesthetic, and historical judgment

The founding of a judgment of musical works on aesthetic

criteria is not so self-evident as it appears to a listener raised in the tradition of the nineteenth century, a tradition which reaches far into the twentieth. The concept of an aesthetic judgment is a historical, and hence variable, category whose origin does not reach back beyond the eighteenth century and which seems to have lost relevance in recent decades. One usually identifies by the crude labels "old" and "new" the music of the epochs surrounding the century and a half generally considered to represent the era of "music proper." Those epochs had characteristic forms of judgment strictly distinguishable from aesthetic judgment and identifiable by the formulas "functional" and "historical."

1. Aesthetic judgment centers on the idea of the musically beautiful, an idea so worn out that historic consciousness must strain to reconstruct what it meant in the nineteenth century. One must not construe the concept too narrowly if one wants to protect it from sinking into commonplace. Significantly, in the nineteenth century one spoke of a "characteristically beautiful" in continually devised systems of aesthetics, and one even tried to draw the ugly as an ingredient into a dialectic of the beautiful. This attitude indicates unmistakably that artistic judgment did not submit itself to a narrow notion of the beautiful but that, on the contrary, the notion of the beautiful depended on artistic feeling and therefore covered a wide field. It would hardly be exaggerating to assert that the category of the beautiful fulfilled in the nineteenth century the same function as the concept of artistic character in the twentieth.

Whereas aesthetic judgment, in Platonic terms, is a pronouncement about the participation or nonparticipation of a musical work in the idea of the beautiful—a judgment whether it is art in the sense of the classic-romantic concept of art—functional judgment, proceeding from sober Aristotelian instead of emphatically Platonic categories, is directed at the appropriateness of a musical piece, at its fitness for the task it is to fulfil. Decisive for *Umgangsmusik* ("music that circulates"), as Heinrich Bessler called it, is whether it seems usable or not. It would be erroneous, to be sure, to define the purpose of functional music of the sixteenth or seventeenth century—liturgical music or secular representative art—on the basis of the narrowed and reduced concept of *Gebrauchsmusik* ("music for use"), which originated only in the late eighteenth and the nineteenth centuries from the splitting-off of autonomous from functional music. If one understands the great art of the sixteenth century as "glorification," then—in contrast to newer notions of *Gebrauchsmusik*—the more artfully composed Mass or political motet is at the same time the more adequate and dignified work according to functional criteria.

Finally, historical judgment, closely connected with the theory and composition practice of the new music, contraposes to the concepts of the beautiful and appropriate, which sustained aesthetic and functional judgments, the category of the "attuned" or the "authentic," which is difficult to grasp. According to Theodor W. Adorno a musical work is *stimmig* ("attuned") when in its technical composition it is the "authentic" expression of what—metaphorically spoken—"the hour calls for historically and philosophically." The contents of meaningful music is not the empirical history but the significance of it for the consciousness and unconsciousness of man. "Attunement" is thus, on one hand, a category of technical composition and, on the other hand, a category of history and philosophy. The concept implies the thesis that technical facts of composition can be read as historic-philosophic signs. The concept defies definition and can be resolved only by the attempt to clarify the thesis it poses through analyses and interpretations.

2. The instructive model for functional judgment in music was the concept of craft. Closely connected with the idea of a function to be fulfilled by a musical work as liturgic motet or as dance was the thought of definite compositional norms which the music had to obey or did not need to obey. One must not translate the word *ars*—which in the Middle Ages and the early Modern Age comprises the concept of art—simply by "craft." The modern categories of craft and art are the result of a split which in the late eighteenth century severed the unity and indivisibleness implied by the concept *ars* into the dualism and contrast of art and craft. (And the original unity can least of all be restored by a *Kunsthandwerk* ["artful piece of workmanship"] that attempts to cancel the separation.)

Aesthetics around 1800 countered the sobriety of an art theory derived from the model of craft by an enthusiastic encroachment upon religious categories. Although a theologian, Herder did not hesitate to describe musical hearing as a state of "devotion."

Wackenroder intensified the devotion to an ecstasy in which the religious sentimentality of the early eighteenth century turned into the aesthetic one of the late century. Compositions were admired, not without blasphemous pretention, as "creations." The concept, too, of "contemplation," placed by Schopenhauer into the center of aesthetics, is unmistakably of religious origin.

The sentiment reconciling religion and aesthetics, which tended to transform temples into museums, and museums into temples, has in the twentieth century, though surviving, become suspect of being a confused and muddy mixture: a distortion of both religion and art. The return to the model of craft, on the the other hand, in the sense of the older unimpaired concept of *ars*— tried by Paul Hindemith and sympathetically appraised even by Stravinsky—is a mere illusion, more reminiscent of Wagner's "master attitude" than of the real sixteenth century. Younger composers therefore exchanged the model of craft for that of science. The development of composing appears as a process in which, analogously to the evolution of a science, the works present themselves as solutions of problems left over by earlier works; each solution evokes—for its part—problems to be coped with in later works, with no end in sight for the dialectics of creating and solving problems.

3. A functional judgment that measures a musical work by the purpose it is meant to fulfill presupposes a cogent theory with firm norms concerning types of musical composition. Before the rise of the idea of an autonomous music in the late eighteenth century, types were grounded in functions—in the role of music accompanying a liturgical act, a dance, or a festive procession—so that a judgment of the extent to which a work fulfilled the concept of a type coincided with a judgment of the appropriateness of the purpose it served.

Whereas in functional music a work is primarily the exemplar of a type—an exemplar which reaches perfection when it projects the marks of the type clearly and purely—in the epoch of aesthetics, in the nineteenth century, a work bases its claim to be considered art on exactly the opposite, on individuality and originality. This individuality finds support and a nourishing substance, it is true, in the tradition of the type to which it belongs, but it also tries to rise above the norms and limits of the type, which are experienced as obstacles. To measure individuality by the deviations from the typical case would be gross; but the undeniable object of the aesthetic judgment since the nineteenth century is the musical work understood, not as an example of a type, but as an individual with its own, unique, and inner preconditions. In modern music, however, the idea of the work—the central category of nineteenth-century aesthetics—seems to be gradually losing relevance. Historical criticism, characteristic of the twentieth century without being predominant, conceives a musical piece not as an isolated work complete in itself but as document of a step in the process of composition, as a partial ingredient of a work in progress. Decisive is not the significance of a work by itself in the aesthetic present but rather the extent to which it enters influentially into the development of musical thought and methods of composition. And in the extreme case, works that do not matter become superfluous.

4. One of the aesthetic criteria so common and trivial as to escape reflection is whether a musical work succumbs to the "avenging spirit of disappearance" or transcends the time of its production and remains in the concert repertory. Such a criterion is inconspicuous by being omnipresent. The semblance, however, of the criterion of survival as self-evident is an illusion; one deals here with a historic, and hence changeable, category. In those centuries when a piece of music was apprehended primarily as the example of a type, it was not the example that survived but the type as a complex of norms and habits. Only in the nineteenth century, when the traditional types gradually disintegrated, the thought established itself that the individual unique work is the actual substance of art which must be passed on. Autonomous music not tied to functions constitutes the pantheon of masterworks (of which Heinrich Schenker saw himself as the guardian against the disintegrating tendencies of the twentieth century). And inasmuch as the notion that a piece of music qualifies as art by surviving presupposes the emphatic ideas of work and art of the nineteenth century, it is endangered by their disintegration. Composers of new music, sensitive to the hollow sound of the word *art* and hence reluctant to present finished works, pay the price: the misfortune (if it is one) of being dead and done with almost at the instance of appearing does not afflict their products by accident but

is founded in their meaning. To be quickly forgotten is a mark that the avant-garde shares with fashion, thereby becoming suspect of being itself a fashion.

5. The change in forms of judgment—the transition from functional to aesthetic to historical criticism—is connected with a change in the criticizing authorities who lay claim to importance and influence. Criticism proceeding from the function served by a piece of music primarily belongs to those who carry on and establish liturgical functions or secular goals—those who have commissioned the piece. Aesthetic judgment, on the other hand, which criticizes works presenting themselves as autonomous art, appertains to the public, be it the real audience or the utopian audience whose alarming daydream Wagner traced in the final scene of *Die Meistersinger*. In the period of aesthetics, the critic appears, at least ideally, as the representative of the public; he becomes its preceptor only when the discrepancy between the ideal and the empirical audience, the difference between the *volonté de tous* and the *volonté générale*, has become too acute. Therefore the type of critic characteristic of the nineteenth century was the educated dilettante, as represented by Rochlitz and Hanslick; and it is no accident that composers like Berlioz, Schumann, and Hugo Wolf, when writing reviews, tried to hide their status as composers and assumed the attitude of the educated dilettante who disdains the musical analysis of which he is not capable and replaces it by poetizing paraphrases. Not a line written by Hugo Wolf reveals that he could read a score.

Whereas aesthetic criticism tended to maintain the appearance of dilettantism as if speaking of one's métier were tactless, the historical criticism of the twentieth century, analyzing the work as document of a stage in the development of compositional methods and musical thought, is compelled, on the contrary, to display elements of professionalism, even when the prerequisites are feeble. Aesthetic judgment is changed into a technological one. The efforts for the readers' sake to conceal the irresistible propensity toward jargon by profuse metaphors do not minimize the present dilemma of criticism either to disregard the nature of its object or to become as esoteric as the works it discusses.

Analysis and paraphrase

Aesthetic criticism in the form of poetizing paraphrase, characteristic of the nineteenth century, resembles a fashion just passed which invites mockery but which is not enough antiquated to be treated with historic objectivity. It is a piece of the dead past without having already become history. Yet reconstruction of what it meant before its decline may not be useless.

The poetizing manner in its original authentic form postulated, on one hand, the thesis (which Schumann shared with Friedrich Schlegel) that the bad could not be criticized, and, on the other hand, the conviction that even the most differentiated technical formal analysis could not touch the essence of music which revealed itself as "poetic" content exclusively to feeling. The idea of the "poetic" in music must not be confused (to avoid crude misunderstandings) with a tendency to underlay the music with a literary program. (The question was argued whether the "poetic" was supported or counteracted by a program.) In the aesthetics of the nineteenth century, in the theory of art by Jean Paul and Friedrich Schlegel which sustained E. T. A Hoffmann and Schumann, "poesy" had a double meaning, referring to poetry as a particular art form besides painting and music but also to the general nature of art shared by the various art forms. In romantic terminology, the difference between "poetic" and "prosaic" music was that between art and not-art; the primary function of aesthetic criticism is to recognize this difference. When E. T. A. Hoffmann and Schumann praised a piece of music as "poetic," they thereby indicated its character as art or, emphatically put, its belonging to the "realm of art." Proof of the musically "poetic" was the "poetic" atmosphere into which the hearer was lifted by a work. Insofar as the hearer was a critic, he attempted to express this atmosphere verbally through a poetizing paraphrase. On the other hand, one could not criticize "prosaic" or trivial music — experienced as bad music without necessarily being badly composed according to obvious technical criteria — because it did not create a poetic atmosphere to supply sentimental poetizing with a starting point and a substance.

Succinctly stated, "poetizing" converted "poesy" understood as the essential character of the art of music into "poetry" understood as a separate literary art form. Less decisive were the metaphors in which the poetizing fancy indulged (the *Klangbilder-talent*, "talent for sonorous images," as Heine called it) than the capacity of a piece of music to evoke at all an atmosphere demanding articulation by a paraphrase however inadequate. The poetizing, a subjective reflex to the poetic content of the music, was intentionally vague and indefinite. Buttressing it with a program— E. T. A. Hoffmann and Schumann were convinced—destroyed rather than clarified the essence one wanted to grasp.

The poetizing manner was the reverse of the distrust of analysis shared in the nineteenth century by composers—Schumann no less than Wagner—with dilettantes. Form and technique, the "mechanics" of music as Schumann called them contemptuously, should not be displayed but rather concealed. Form was considered the outer skin of music or a means best fulfilling its end by remaining inconspicuous: nothing else but the formulation of a sentence, the perfection of which consists in being forgotten in favor of the contents it transmits.

In the twentieth century, however, the "mechanical" attained aesthetic honors under the name of "structure." The postulate of inconspicuousness was displaced by that of conspicuousness of the means. The focusing on structure implies the concession that technical analysis of composition reaches aesthetic essentials. Upon analysis in the twentieth century devolves the function fulfilled in the nineteenth by the poetizing paraphrase: to establish or at least to clarify the aesthetic judgment whether a piece of music is art.

Moral implications

The irrelevance of morality in art seems self-evident. Ever since Kant in his *Kritik der Urteilskraft* declared judgment of taste, the decision between beautiful and ugly, as "without interest," moral and cognitive interests have remained excluded from aesthetics. True, inquiry concerning the function of music—the utility it has or the damage it does—is ineradicable; but whoever insists on it, unpersuaded that it is queer, feels himself exposed to the disagreeable suspicion of being a Philistine.

To avoid gross misunderstandings, the judgment of taste analyzed by Kant must be distinguished from the judgment of art, from art criticism. According to Kant, a work of art is not exhausted by being an aesthetic object, the aim of a judgment of taste. Insofar as it transmits a content and accompanies or represents an affect or an action, it also comprehends moral elements which, merely by their attachment to a work of art, do not cease to be accessible to moral "interest." The judgment of taste as understood by Kant is a mere ingredient of art criticism; and in contrast to the former, the latter cannot possibly be disinterested. The moral implications of works of art were as obvious to Kant as they were to Schiller, when he pronounced his questionable verdict on Bürger.

The separation of elements, which even in theory is not so unambiguous as it appears to a rigorism erroneously calling upon Kant, is in reality totally fictitious. One need not expect of a morality which tries to interfere with the course of the world the forbearance to concede to art a world by itself. On the other hand, a *l'art pour l'art* attitude always tends toward becoming aestheticism, which replaces or colors moral decisions by aesthetic ones. Reflecting on art and morals, one is entangled in the dialectics that the decision to exclude morality from the debate on art is in itself a moral decision.

While a rigorous separation of morality from aesthetics thus appears difficult in reality or even impossible, an intellectual distinction of the elements and an analysis of the interplay are indispensable. The dichotomy to be explored and illuminated reaches down to fundamental concepts of aesthetics, which, upon reflection, prove to be mixed concepts.

1. The category of originality, which became in the late eighteenth century the definitive aesthetic authority, implies as the opposite of imitation and convention the postulate that a work of art worthy of the name must be substantially new. On the other hand, the concept of originality—especially in its literal meaning of pertaining to an origin—evokes the association with something immediate and unpremeditated. One looks for the "origin" of the new, signified by the word "originality," in simple feelings. Yet the two conceptual elements do not exactly coincide. The opinion that feeling and not reflection is the authority responsible for the new in

music history leads to an erroneous prejudice. Precisely the works of composers whose originality was evident and even disturbing to their contemporaries—Monteverdi, Berlioz, or Schönberg—for all their intense determination by emotions undeniably bear the stamp of reflection. What Schütz praised in Monteverdi was his *Scharfsinn* ("sagacity").

The mistrust of reflection is thus less aesthetically than morally motivated. Moralists often regard the secondary, reflective impulse with suspicion, convinced that it distorts the primary, more humane one by pragmatic considerations. But in art theory—we do not speak of the musical entertainment industry, in which pragmatism prevails—skepticism toward the reflection praised by Jean Paul as prudence (a skepticism shared by Schumann and Pfitzner with dilettantes who worship anything original) appears as the result of a false transfer. The primary thought is generally the more self-conscious one, dependent upon conventions, habits, and concerns. And not seldom is it a calculated ploy through which a composer outwits the traditionalism in himself.

2. More clearly than in the case of the postulate of originality, the moral implications of the aesthetic judgment reveal themselves in the concept of the "genuine." In Nietzsche's, the moralist's, criticism of Wagner, the concept played a role as decisive as it was questionable before subsequently sinking into a commonplace, which served primarily as justification of provincial obtuseness. In popular aesthetics, of which it became the guiding principle, the "genuine" forms the contrast and counterpart to the "fabricated," to aesthetic calculation suspect of fraud. Already Nietzsche tended to suspect the aesthetically legitimate appearance as morally illegitimate and to convert the tautology that theater, even as *Bühnenfestspiel* ("stage festival play") or *Bühnenweihfestspiel* ("stage consecration festival play"), remains theater into a reproach against Wagner. In the idea of the genuine, which is an aesthetic-moral mixture, heterogeneous and even contradictory elements indeed intertwine. In the language of those who use the word as a slogan, "genuine" indicates the original as opposed to mere imitation, the slowly grown as opposed to quick construction decried as "mechanical," and the sentimental as opposed to the thoughtful; but it also indicates the habitual as opposed to the foreign, and the

old and traditional in contrast to a modernity seen through paranoia as "fraud." With all the confusion surrounding the contents of the concept, the function it fulfils is unambiguous: it is always, and independently of the gradations and discolorations of its meaning, a conservative and secretly polemic category. And contrary to the tendency to denounce "made" things as "not genuine," modern poetry and art theory, of which the beginnings reach back to Poe and Baudelaire, insist on the maxim that poems are "made." In the words of Mallarmé, whose extreme sensitivity caused him to lean toward provocative sobriety, poems are made not of feelings or ideas but of words. Characteristically, the concept of calculation or construction, an invective in the aesthetics of the genuine, has become a positive category.

3. The English literary critic Matthew Arnold, not without malice but with illuminating exaggeration, characterized art of the middle class as *kitsch*, and that of the lower class as trash. The aesthetic difference appears as sign of a social difference. Without bothering to define *kitsch* and trash—the vague general understanding of the words suffices—one is obliged to notice that the judgment on both kinds or strata of trivial art has undergone a change in the twentieth century. In the nineteenth (as its attribution to the middle class indicates), it was *kitsch* which was aesthetically tolerated or even counted as art; it supplied, so to speak, the realization of several popular prejudices concerning art. Trash, on the other hand, openly parading its primitive and vulgar features while appearing variegated and enticing, provoked resistance and aversion, in which aesthetic motives mixed with social and moral ones. Trash had to be kept at a distance. In the twentieth century, however, one has become increasingly sensitized to *kitsch*—in extreme cases, to the point of persecutory intolerance. The invention and establishment of the word *kitsch* both express the distrust and reinforce it. Simultaneously, criticism of trash has diminished, for various reasons which do not all fit together. The aesthetic distance to the art of the avant-garde is too great and too obvious to need elaboration; the social difference is not cancelled but rather denied, because aesthetic. education appears as a privilege enjoyed with a bad or at least morbid conscience; and the morally suspect or disreputable qualities of trash are considered

irrelevant or are even pointed out. The attempts, finally, to mediate between avant-garde and musical trash are informative precisely because of their fruitlessness: the less factually backed and legitimized they are by technical aspects of the compositions, the more clearly and openly they reveal the moral and socio-psychological tendencies by which they are moved.

Historic-philosophic categories

The concept of a musical work as a "world in itself," typical of romantic art theory, implies the thought that music which has attained classicism removes itself from history. The idea, however, of an aesthetic judgment which abstracts from the period in which the works originated is utopian in a bad sense: a caricature of the judgment *sub specie aeternitatis.* Musical criticism dissatisfied with merely paraphrasing the "Ah and Oh of sentiment," as Hegel called it, cannot renounce categories like *new* and *epigonal,* of which the historic implications are patent without exposing or condemning itself to shrinkage.

But in a qualitative and not merely chronological sense, not everything deviating from the habitual belongs to the new. Newness as an aesthetic criterion is a perplexing historic-philosphic category.

First, the idea of something new evokes the image of a beginning, of a caesura in history, signifying or apparently signifying a break with tradition. Works and methods of composition that offer a continuation of something earlier by having sprung up from a tradition in continuous transition are never experienced as emphatically new even when they eventually lead far out into the unknown and unpredictable. True novelty, in the case of Monteverdi no less than Berlioz or Schönberg, involves a trait of violence and of delight in destruction.

Second, anything new must be topical. It must appear as an expression of what is timely in a historic-philosophic sense. Anybody going astray at the periphery, like Josef Matthias Hauer, is condemned to sectarianism. (And it would be wrong to see only a sociological category in the concept of a sect. According to sociological criteria, the "Schönberg clique," as its adversaries called it, was also a sect.) While it is questionable to speak of the timeliness of an event that remains hidden and thus is not really an event, timeliness itself does not at all depend on success (or spectacular failure); a conspicuous (and thus actually unsuccessful) boycott suffices. Nobody, not even an unswerving conservative like Alfred Heuss, doubted after 1910 the timeliness of Schönberg's music, of which its very opponents felt the importance.

Third, in historical retrospect a work or event appears new only when one can ascribe to it an effect lasting beyond the present, beyond the moment of timeliness. Without Monteverdi who, by drawing compositional consequences from the rudimentary first attempts of the Camerata, became the real founder of opera as the central genre of the epoch, the Florentine *dramma per musica* would have remained a peripheral experiment—one of the countless cumulative attempts in the sixteenth century to restore antique music: petrifactions of a dissipated enthusiasm.

The concept of epigonism—an opposite and contrasting foil to newness and originality—is a category of the nineteenth century which earlier periods would hardly have understood. Imitation of models and stylistic copies, in the time of sentimental aesthetics morally and aesthetically suspect of "lack of genuineness" and of routine in the worst sense of the word, were considered indispensable as well as legitimate until the early eighteenth century. They were actually signs of the solidity of the technical foundation of composition and showed piety toward tradition. Nobody interpreted them as a shameful lack of intellectual capacity.

Epigonism is traditionalism become suspect. It fell into disrepute in the nineteenth century and was labeled *Kapellmeister music* because of changed views of a musical work. The dependence on models was a matter of course in earlier centuries when, under the domination of traditional musical types, the individual work was primarily understood as an example of a type to whose norms it conformed. As soon, however, as a work appears no longer as the representative of a type but as an individual unique piece, imitation, an offense against uniqueness, falls under a cloud.

Split and ambivalent is the relation of epigonism to historicism as musical practice and as theory: to the historic treatment of concert and opera repertories and to the differentiation of historical consciousness. Somehow historicism and epigonism seem to exclude or contradict each other. The historical approach to musical practice and the almost uninterrupted survival of old music have rendered imitation of older models superfluous. While Beethoven's compositions, although expressions of a dead past, dominate the musical present, there is no room for Beethoven epigones who would be mere shadow figures. And historical consciousness works in the same direction inasmuch as it is consciousness of the strangeness of the past. The more acutely developed the feeling for historic differences and for whatever was "timely" at any period, the more sensitively it reacts against the "lack of contemporaneity" of epigonal works. A historian trying to fend off the transfer to the past of current habits of thought ought, on the other hand, to be suspicious of the encroachment of the past on the present.

But historicism and epigonism mutually support and influence each other. The overgrowth by the past of the present musical repertory makes epigonism superfluous, as noted above, but at the same time also challenges it. Imitation of musical models in the seventeenth and eighteenth centuries lacked strict fidelity because, among other reasons, one was not very well acquainted with the models which, except for a few leftovers, had disappeared from the active repertory. In the nineteenth century, however, composers knew older music so well that at least the weaker ones among them involuntarily relapsed into accustomed procedures even while trying to avoid them. Nobody can escape the omnipresence of the musical past. In the nineteenth century, historic consciousness both hindered and stimulated style copies of older music. The enthusiasm for the musical past, rising above its strangeness, generated sympathy toward attempts at restoration instead of insight into the historic-philosophic impossibility of such attempts.

Epigonism, the dependence on canonized prototypes, must be distinguished from the superannuation of antiquated pieces which, pushed out of the center, occasionally survive tenaciously on the periphery of an epoch. Epigonism involves lack of historic consequences (except for the epigones of epigones), whereas antiquated music, after apparent condemnation by history, sometimes found itself suddenly reinterpreted as modern or discovered as significant for the future.

A paradigm is the modern "free" counterpoint of the early seventeenth century, the center of the theory of rhetorical musical "figures." In the fifteenth and sixteenth centuries, the development of counterpoint in the centers of music history tended toward restriction: limitation and regulation of the use of dissonances were considered progressive, not regressive. The rigorism of Tinctoris or Gafurius characterized theories that looked ahead, not limped behind. In the early seventeenth century, however, the breaking of norms became a criterion of modern counterpoint. Deviations from the rules were legitimized as means of an emphatic representation of the text, as rhetorical musical figures. In the period of transition, the tendencies nevertheless intermixed. In the case of composers like Byrd or Morley, one can sometimes hardly decide whether a dissonant figure is "still" archaic or "already" modern.

To cite another extreme example, Arnold Schönberg's historical position in the decades in which neoclassicism determined the musical present was also ambivalent. In retrospect, one can be convinced of the validity of the prevailing opinion in the 1920s and 30s that Schönberg's music was an antiquated "last stage of romanticism." The change of opinion in the 1940s then appears as a reinterpretation of something old as something modern. Or one can believe that Schönberg's compositional procedures were "timely" also in the 20s and 30s and that the semblance of historic representativeness of neoclassicism was but an illusion.

Aesthetics and investigations of reception

Skeptics who stubbornly doubt the possibility of an objective and factually grounded aesthetic judgment occasionally place complete confidence—as if they were weary and tired of their own skepticism—in the prospects of an empirical investigation "without preconditions" of the reception of music. Aesthetics suspect of forays into metaphysics ought to be displaced or replaced, to put it pointedly, by research into reception. Without wishing to deny the utility of such investigations and their right to exist, one must recognize that they have to be based on aesthetics if they wish to avoid absurdity. (It is difficult, in any case, to accept the solution of the Gordian knot as a model for scientific procedure.)

1. The method of investigating musical reception by gathering and counting opinions about musical pieces must, in order not to conclude in a void, presuppose that aesthetic judgments are based on sufficient similarity of the musical perceptions. But such a supposition, as the most casual analysis can show, is flawed or even fictitious. Musical habits of hearing are too diverse to let one admit that statistics based on chance selection of subjects for the experiment are a collection of opinions on the same issue. The possibility to compare and count is not inherently given but must first be realized. Because musical pieces are objects of an "artificial" reception acquired through cultural traditions, and not of a "natural" reception, the similarity or dissimilarity of musical perceptions depends on the degree of insight into the structure of music. Without an examination—at least in the rough—of the factual musical judgment underlying an aesthetic judgment, the latter cannot be statistically registered.

2. Empirical investigation of reception considers as suspect or uncomfortable the by no means "metaphysical" concept of the "qualified" hearer, whose aesthetic judgment rests on a sufficiently adequate factual judgment, because it would have to take him over from the outside, from musical analysis and aesthetics. It therefore tends to interpret the difference between listeners who understand the form and structure of a musical work and those who do not as a mere difference of "group norms" and to ignore it. The thesis that the "group norm" of pop-tune fans to whom Beethoven symphonies seem confused and boring has an aesthetic right to exist equal to the "group norm" of Beethoven enthusiasts who dismiss a hit tune as monotonous and trivial—this thesis is just as "metaphysical" as the antithesis that it does not have it. (The social right to exist is not under discussion.) The seeming dispensation from preconditions is a fallacy. The investigation of musical reception substitutes a "democratic" prejudice which it does not unmask as prejudice for the "aristocratic" one which it considers disreputable. Underlying

is the conviction that all judgments, also the least informed, have the same aesthetic weight. The consequence is a registration of opinions. That "quantification" is superior to "qualification" and representative of progressive methods is less established in aesthetics than in the natural sciences, which empirical-statistical investigation of reception emulates.

3. As long as investigation of reception tries to avoid aesthetics, it suffers from the deficiency or confusion of collecting and counting opinions without having adequately defined the objective. It leaves open whether the musical piece presented to the participants in the experiment is to be interpreted as mere entertainment or as an aesthetic object. The decision that it is an aesthetic object would mean the exclusion from the experiment of a listener incapable of constituting an aesthetic object. The referral back to mere entertainment, on the other hand, which investigation of reception favors to avoid losing its way in the labyrinths of aesthetics, is by no means "neutral." The dissolution of musical form into an ensemble of isolated stimuli next to each other like spots of color is rather a mark of trivial music or of trivial hearing. A theory resorting to the stimulation involved without regard to the success, failure, or absence of the attempt to constitute an aesthetic object is thus rather a hidden apology for musical banality than an aesthetically "unprejudiced" investigation of reception.

4. The claim that habits of hearing and their social premises are too varied among randomly selected test subjects to ground aesthetic judgments on musical observations of sufficient similarity is exposed to the objection that significant music is characteristically "multivalent." It can be heard on different levels of understanding without losing its sense and effect on the lower levels. Works like *The Magic Flute* or *The Creation* are directed at the naive as well as the reflective hearer. As persuasive as it seems, however, this argument is only half true; the criterion of "multivalence" in its relevance and scope is historically restricted to the period of classicism. In the romantic period, the relationship between exoteric and reflective esoteric elements of music became a problem. For Liszt, it turned into a dilemma. In modern music, the unity of the popular and the esoteric, notwithstanding incessant efforts to restore it, has completely fallen apart, probably forever.

The notion of a classicism of modern music would be paradoxical; extension of the criterion of "multivalence" to music of the later nineteenth and of the twentieth centuries seems a false generalization and a provocation to polemical abuse of the category. Nobody denies that the time around 1800 was a happy moment in the history of music; but the danger is not slight that yearning for the past may turn into hating one's own present.

Criteria

On the logic of aesthetic judgment

The language in which aesthetic judgments are formulated is often vague and confused. Logical purists obsessed by a desire to lock all ideas into fixed definitions should avoid aesthetics and its history, which would drive them to despair. The complaint about terminological chaos—a chaos steadily increased by innovations and strict definitions meant to dam it—has become the kind of cliché by which historians express their awareness of the theoretic deficiencies of their scholarly discipline. Nevertheless, they cannot improve it. While historians certainly have the task of analyzing equivocal concepts, the enforcement of terminological uniformity by abbreviating and reducing the contents of the traditional language of aesthetics would be an error. Even with its pervading tears and splits, that language is still a historic document.

1. The concept of "originality"—since the late eighteenth century one of the supportive categories of aesthetics—is a double concept. The two elements it contains—the presentation of the immediate and nonreflective and that of the new and unpredictable—are, as stated earlier, not always reconcilable. A historian would waste his time trying to reduce the vague and wide concept to a narrow and unambivalent term. The idea of originality has become historically effective precisely as an equivocal category. An updated use of words which abstracts from history for the sake of logic would shrink the concept to a shadow of its former self.

Even more complicated are the implications of the concept of genuineness, which as an aesthetic category is both dubious and ineradicable. Diverse and heterogeneous elements become intertwined: the degradation of dependence on models to an aesthetically suspect epigonism; the expectation that music be the sincere expression of the composer's emotions; the image of reliable craft, firmly rooted and removed from the vagaries of fashion which tends toward "fraud"; finally, the orientation to a tradition of musical types, such as a "genuine" song type or "genuine" church music. The contradictions splitting the concept are obvious but do not reduce its significance. The historian's task is not to reconcile the contradictions or to eliminate them by restricting the concept but to understand them as marks of the epoch in which the advancement of "genuineness" to an aesthetic catchword was not just an accident.

2. There seems to be no remedy for the confusion generated by the admission of contrary or differently colored aesthetic judgments of the same technical and stylistic facts of composition — the leaning on a model or the deviating from a tradition of forms and types. The dependence of musical works on models to be imitated or emulated may be praised as expression of an unbroken feeling for tradition or condemned as epigonism withdrawing from the aesthetic demands of the day. The combining and mingling of heterogeneous technical and stylistic premises of composition appears either as successful synthesis or as fractured eclecticism with no aesthetic right to exist. The verdict of a polemicist who suspects the "open form" of a work deviating from tradition as "ruptured" can always be countered easily by the judgment of an apologist who justifies "ruptured" forms as "open."

There is no authority with jurisdiction to decide what to count as traditionalism and what as epigonism. The arbitrariness of shades of judgment can be minimized, however, by attempts to determine contradictory criteria historically and thus to limit their scope. The concept of epigonism, as mentioned earlier, is a characteristic category of the nineteenth century which would be anachronistic if blindly applied to music of earlier centuries. And conversely, tradition and feeling for tradition, which were a matter of course in the seventeenth and still in the eighteenth centuries, became an object of reflection and restoration in the nineteenth because they were seen as endangered.

In an analogous manner, the remaining criteria can be treated historically. Synthesis of heterogeneous traditions is not always a judicious possibility. Without violent effort (almost always a sign of fruitlessness), it seems to succeed primarily in times of a musical classicism, such as the sixteenth and the late eighteenth centuries. On the other hand, in an epoch as far removed from classics and classicism as the twentieth century, any talk of synthesis (and there prevails a superabundance rather than a shortage of syntheses) arouses the suspicion that mere eclecticism is to be masked by a sonorous vocable (which, anyway, has gradually turned hollow through misuse).

3. Aesthetic criteria can rarely be isolated without losing relevance and color. They do not stand by themselves but rather show their significance and scope only in complexes of arguments in which they mutually complement, support, restrict, or confront each other. Separated from one another, they turn into the vague and impalpable schemes decried by detractors of aesthetics.

Thus a wealth of connections is not relevant in every case to aesthetic judgment but only when the parts to be related are characteristically diverse. In a melodic line without character, everything seems connected with everything; but one deals here less with a wealth of connections than with a lack of differentiations. Abundance of interrelations becomes a valid aesthetic criterion only as a counterpart to the characteristic and distinct design of the things related.

4. Whereas wealth of motivic connections can be (but must not always be) a quality relevant to the aesthetic criticism of a work, lack of motivic connections does not necessarily indicate a deficiency. (There are also other means of producing coherence.) Absence of a criterion does not force reversal of the judgment. A negative decision—the reproach of insufficient coherence or integration—is adequately sustained only by the demonstration that the deficient feature would be aesthetically necessary as complement and counterpart of a given property. Little or weak integration of a musical text is not by itself a deficiency reducing the aesthetic value of the work, but it becomes one in the case of extensive differentiations which it ought to be able to bring into agreement.

5. Aesthetic criteria, singly or jointly, never offer sufficient support for judgment of a musical work. Any attempt to base music criticism on flawless rationality would have to run aground or lose itself in sectarianism. But the limitation and inadequacy of rational judgment do not permit one to conclude that it is impotent and submissive to the irrationality of a taste judgment. There is no cause for letting one's self be intimidated by the pretension of irrationalism which nestles down in the interstices of knowledge and then asserts that the dark remains not reached by reason are the uniquely decisive factor. Aesthetics surrenders by making concessions to the enemies of rationality and reflection.

"Badly composed" and trivial music

Erroneous prejudice or at least crude exaggeration characterizes the opinion that trivial music, from the salon piece to the hit tune, from the periphery of operetta to entertainment music, is in a tangible sense "badly composed" and that uncovering technical deficiencies of a composition suffices to convict "lower music" of aesthetic wretchedness. One may detest as *kitsch* Gounod's "Ave Maria" in which piety presents itself as a salon attitude, or one may become indignant over the abuse of the C-major Prelude by Bach. In terms of compositional technique, however, the piece is impeccable. Whoever dismisses it as "badly composed" betrays an aesthetic-moral embarrassment which muddies and distorts factual musical criticism. The "Ave Maria," like the plays of Scribe, belong to the *pièces bien faites* over which one need not fly into a passion; they are too good to arouse anger, and too bad to deserve it.

The concept of "well-composed," however, does not mean the same at all times; it became confused and vague precisely in the nineteenth century. Not only the code of technical norms, but also the relevance generally granted the concept of "well-composed" is subject to historical fluctuations. Whereas in earlier periods the emulation of firmly established models sufficed, since the late eighteenth century any composer adhering to fixed rules has been suspected of pedantry and epigonism.

Impeccable composition of a piece according to the letter of the laws of the *Conservatoire* is thus no protection against triviality or *kitsch;* but to be praised as significant, on the other hand, a work apparently need not always be "well-composed." Or more precisely: in the nineteenth century the concept of "well-composed" loses the firm outlines it showed earlier. Nobody denies the inadequacy of measuring works by Berlioz or Liszt by the code represented by Cherubini. Uncertain, however, is the question whether the catastrophe of the irruption of Berlioz's *Symphonie fantastique* into music history established new upside-down norms of "well-composed" or whether it caused the category of "well-composed" to forfeit its aesthetic relevance. In the nineteenth century, an apologist for the "music of the future" had the choice either of sacrificing the concept of "well-composed" and relinquishing it to the conservatives (the "cantors," as Schumann called them) or of adopting and usurping it for whatever the avant-garde composed. It is truly a usurpation inasmuch as the idea of incessant progress represented by an avant-garde is irreconcilable with the tendency, prerequisite for the formation of the "well-composed" norm, toward stabilization of what has been technically accomplished in composition. The paradoxical notion of an individual norm—the postulate that a work cannot be measured by anything except its own implied measure—signifies an abolition of the category "well-composed" in the traditional sense.

The domain of the "well-composed," which seems faultless according to norms of musical craft but questionable or of no account according to aesthetics, extends from dances and marches of "solid texture" (a matter of good conscience in the nineteenth and early twentieth centuries) to functional liturgic music clinging to the idol of the Palestrina style (as if avoidance of accented passing dissonances were a musical form of purity and asceticism). The aesthetic right to exist, doubted by no one, which the Palestrina style as the *stile antico* had in the seventeenth and eighteenth centuries, has become sickly since the nineteenth century under the rule of the romantic concept of art. True, the aesthetic-religious reverence with which one regarded old music inspired imitation and pious reproductions in which the purity of the conviction was exemplified by that of the counterpoint. But imitation and emulating piety were aesthetically suspect of violating the postulate of originality and individual musical expression. Thus Cecilianism, the Palestrina style turned dogma, shared with its extreme opposite, salon and dance music, the fate of sinking into triviality, into a genre not protected from the criticism of being "bad music" by being "well-composed."

The aesthetic and technical concepts of "good" and "bad" music no longer fit together and even pull in opposite directions. Questions arise. Is a piece in Palestrina style, a Mass or motet in the "old style," around 1900 still "well-composed" music? Is such a piece really a composition in the undiluted sense of the word and not rather a school exercise betraying, like so many linguistic formations, its origin in the spirit of grammar and not of poetry? Is for the concept of "well-composed" the alternative unavoidable of either clinging to fixed and finally petrified norms or—by a switch into the opposite extreme—dissolving into a synonym for the compositional methods of the avant-garde of the moment, an avant-garde of which the representative can only be determined in retrospect? Can music emancipated from tradition and removed from the traditional code of rules still be "well-composed" in a technically tangible sense, and not just in the vague historic-philosophic sense that places it at the real or apparent peak of the development?

Paradigms of new music going against rules yet immediately recognized as "well-composed" are the works of Debussy, the "anti-dilettante," who, while a revolutionary, detested anything abrupt. One of the reasons for the impression of technical impeccability is clearly one's experiencing the departures from the traditional norms, not as isolated violations of the customary (like the inversion of a ninth chord in Schönberg's *Transfigured Night* that offended a Viennese jury), but as so closely interconnected as almost to form a system. To put it paradoxically: what singly and scattered would be a technical and aesthetic deficiency becomes legitimized by exaggeration, by the consistency with which it recurs, and by the interconnection with other elements of the piece. Because a deeply incisive and consistent deviation from the norm is aesthetically more persuasive than a slight one without consequences, the "moderately modern" in new music appears as excessive timidity rather than as an expression of prudence, which Jean Paul praised as the highest aesthetic virtue.

In order not to appear aesthetically inconsequential, music violating the established norms of the "well-composed" must be at least both stylistically advanced and technically self-consistent. And conversely, it is a criterion of the musically poor or defective that deviations from the technical code of rules indicate a relapse and that they are disconnected details perceived as accidental breaks in the texture. One must not be fooled if the marks of bad music sometimes are not deficiencies due to incompetence or sloppiness but rather calculated stimuli. Even when exposed as masked cynicism, musical stupidity does not cease to be annoying or unbearable.

The reverse of the emphatic-romantic concept of art is the creation of trivial music which need not be "badly composed" to incur aesthetic contempt. To the extent to which Wackenroder and Tieck, E. T. A. Hoffmann and Schumann had elevated the metaphysical dignity of music to immeasurable heights, music not fulfilling the task of being sonorous poetry was endangered in its very aesthetic existence. It appeared either as "prosaic" music, as Schumann called it, or as *kitsch* (for which a definition was still lacking in the nineteenth century). Functional music, accepted in earlier periods without aesthetic reflections, became suspect under the rule of the romantic art concept of selling out as "prose" music destined for "poetry." The "*Kapellmeister* music" of the nineteenth century is not badly composed compared to that of the eighteenth; but measured by the emphatic-romantic concept of music, it sounded hollow and insignificant.

"Prosaic" music is thus trivial without denying it, whereas *kitsch* is created, as it were, by aesthetic usurpation. It is "prosaic" music disguised as "poetic." It fails when reaching for the summit, when attempting to acquire the character of art without compositional foundation for aesthetic demands and attitudes. Triviality, which was meant to be hidden, appears all the more shabby when uncovered. *Kitsch* is the parvenu of art.

Abundance of relationships

John Cage's dadaism illustrates, rather than obliterates, the commonplace that music is a coherence of tones. The attempt to sever the connection between adjoining acoustical phenomena to make the detail audible "for itself" and not as part and function of a whole presupposes as common norm—to produce surprise through which alone the isolated becomes conspicuous—precisely the apperception of connections. The separation and isolation, the severing of habitual connections, are difficult. They succeed only in rare moments, rightly felt by Cage as mystical now. The engrained connections, however, against which the resistance and the practicing polemics of dadaism are directed must be differentiated from the melodic-rhythmic relationships within a single work. The variability and density of such relationships belong to the aesthetic criteria of compositional technique which survived almost unimpaired the breaks in tradition around 1910 and 1950. In the aesthetically relevant sense, abundance of relationships is not general and fixed but rather the particular coherence in a single work. Negatively expressed: the less individuality there is in a piece of music, the smaller the aesthetic significance of the relations between the parts. The polemics against cohesion in music—felt to be a coercion—misses its target by confusing the abundance of relationships tied to the particularity of a unique work with the engrained elements of unification unacceptable in the violent drive toward loose anarchy.

Musical abundance of relationships is a fact that cannot be read from the notation without further propositions. It reveals itself only as the result of analyses or interpretations proceeding from changing, historically variable principles which one may accept or reject. Thus there is controversy surrounding the Bach analyses by Johann Nepomuk David and the Beethoven analyses by Rudolf Réti; and whether they are discoveries of hidden connections or unreal constructions has not been established. Aesthetic judgment thus depends on a factual judgment which in turn includes an aesthetic decision about the validity or invalidity of the premises underlying the analyses.

The circle, however, is not vicious, for one can name several conditions that have to be met for musical coherence to be both real and aesthetically relevant. The first postulate is for a piece to be of sharply defined character. The appearance of motivic relationships is an illusion if the themes or melodic figures which one relates to each other are not sufficiently characteristic. The hypothesis, that in early classical symphonies the first and last movements are related through their thematic "substance," has been rightly challenged on the grounds that the generic similarity of symphonic themes around 1780 is so great that the specific similarity of single themes lacks definite marks. The degree of correspondence defining motivic relationship is different in the eighteenth century from what it is in the nineteenth.

Second, motivic interplays become aesthetically relevant only when they do not remain isolated and peripheral, appearing as chance or fleeting associations, but when they cast a net of inter-relations over an entire movement, determining the structure of a work. Using a formula, one could speak of a postulate of consistency.

Third, the procedure of tying ever closer connections presupposes—apart from the adequately defined features of melodic characters—a degree of complication justifying the toil of "motivic work." Dodecaphony, the extreme of thematic-motivic intertwining, is meaningful and adequate only as a counterpart to the melodic behavior that tends to crumble (in the wake of the "emancipation of dissonance" which influenced melody as much as harmony).

Characteristic of analysts in the twentieth century is the ambition to discover a system of relationships hidden behind the acoustic skin of a musical work, behind the façade it presents to a superficial hearer. This ambition was absent in earlier periods. The question remains as to whether the application to older music of methods that have been developed is adequate or anachronistic. They proceed by abstraction that initially seems violent. In the course of decades, however, they have become such a confirmed habit that one's attention is barely disturbed anymore by the separation of the pitch sequence, the diastematics, from rhythm, although pitch sequence is not an independent element and has no real perceptible existence without duration. The latent connections in a musical work discovered by analysts are declared to be the "scaffolding" or "ground plan," consisting generally of nothing else but the agreement of tone sequences if one disregards rhythm and position within the measure. (Abstraction, which seemed to Wilhelm Dyckerhoff in the nineteenth century a scurrilous experiment with a scalpel, has become in the twentieth the predominant method.)

Although theory is not always dependent on compositional practice and explicable as its reflex in musical thought, the severing and emancipating of an inherently dependent partial element of music is a characteristic which analytic technique shares with Schönberg's and Webern's serial composition. Schönberg's influence on Rudolf Réti is obvious. August Halm and Heinrich Schenker, however, developed independently of each other their abstracting methods before Schönberg "discovered" or "invented" serial technique. They were even, crudely categorized, musical conservatives; new music was viewed by Halm with diffidence, by Schenker with polemic irritation. Yet there is a hidden affinity with serial technique which, not dissimilarly to Halm's demonstrations of motivic connections or Schenker's *Urlinien*, considers pitch sequences by themselves without rhythm.

Methods of abstraction are undeniably anachronistic when used to interpret Bach or Beethoven, because the concept of parameter—separate courses for pitch and duration—was as foreign to the eighteenth and nineteenth centuries as the term. This fact, however, does not imply that they are inadequate or ineffective. Abstraction is one of the forms through which musical thought of the twentieth century appropriates tradition. It is as legitimate or illegitimate as traditions always have been that mix piety and unscrupulousness. One can hardly decide on an empirical basis whether the results of an abstracting procedure are "discoveries" or "reinterpretations," because the definition of the "objective content" in a musical work to be "discovered" remains uncertain. Is it what the composer intended, or what his contemporaries apperceived, or is it the essence distilled from all interpretations which—even when seemingly anachronistic—at least meet the condition of not contradicting the letter of the text and of being by themselves sensible and coherent?

Thus the method of abstraction, leading to the uncovery or construction of rich melodic relationships, is preceded by an aesthetic decision, namely, that the separation of pitch sequence and rhythm is sensible and not absurd. Analysis and aesthetic judgment mesh and support each other. Abundance of relationships, however, remains aesthetically irrelevant—a construction in a void—if the music in which far-reaching and complicated relationships spread throughout is not sufficiently articulated. In recent years, the concept of articulation has unfortunately become a catchword that hampers aesthetic reflection and that shares with other such words the quality of seeming precise as long as one does not think about it but proving itself vague when one tries to grasp it exactly.

"Articulation" is a double concept, an equivocal term, designating, on one hand, the similarity to language and expressiveness of music and, on the other hand, its clear, observable, formal organization. Music is considered "articulate" when the melodic invention is persuasive, and at the same time the form (the syntactic and functional distinction of parts) is apperceptible. These two elements do not always agree without discord; for convincing formal organization is usually provided by the schematic and the habitual whereas musical expressiveness and similarity to language are tied to a departure from the ingrained. "Articulation"—if the ambivalence of the term may be interpreted as sign of dialectics inherent in the situation—is an idea containing the demand for the reconciliation of opposite tendencies: music must say new things without becoming unclear, and it must remain discernible without relapsing into conventionality.

Differentiation and integration

It is a law of biology (inviting transfer to art) that differentiation and integration—manifold distinction of the parts of a whole and their closer functional cohesion—are two aspects of the same development which engage and complement each other. Whether this law operates in aesthetics as empirical rule or as postulate, and whether its historical scope is unlimited or restricted, has not been settled. Without aesthetic and historic reflection, praise of growing differentiation and stricter integration is, in any case, hardly valid. It would be both idle and easy to enumerate richly differentiated musical works which show a low degree of integration: the series would extend from Gregorian melodies governed by the principle of *varietas,* non-repetition, to the "obligatory recitative" in Schönberg's *Orchestra Pieces* op. 16. An aesthetic law analogous to the biological law is out of the question.

But even as an aesthetic postulate, the principle of conciliating differentiation and integration is not always defensible. Compared to a chain of variations in gallant style, of which the separate pieces seem exchangeable and are set apart from one another merely by changing patterns of figuration, a classical variation cycle indeed forms a higher grade of evolution which may be described as the result of interlocking differntiation and integration; here the parts each have a clearly distinctive character and function and thus project instead of a mere chain a molded and closed total form. Yet one doubts whether Schönberg's and Webern's early atonal works, extremely differentiated without the compensation of an analogously developed integration, therefore suffer from an aesthetic deficiency removed only later by dodecaphony. Apparently the biological analogy fails in certain periods. The spontaneous suspicion arises that the postulate of the complementation of differentiation and integration—like other aesthetic conceptions based on an organic model—hides a classicistic tendency which leads to injustice toward stylistically archaic or mannered works. The classsicistically colored argument which seeks to ascribe aesthetic-historic necessity to dodecaphony is countered by a feeling for musical form which recognizes in early atonality—notwithstanding the weak integration in some works—a condition with its own proper aesthetic rights.

Although integration is thus not a postulate of unrestricted and historically invariable validity and scope, one can hardly deny that the drive toward ever stricter and comprehensive integration belongs to the tendencies which have determined the course of music history, at least in Europe, if not without interruptions and relapses. The separate elements of musical texture—mensural rhythm, chromatic alteration of steps, melodic figures and ornaments, dynamics and timbre—have at different times been introduced into notation, the musical text, and hence been integrated with the composition (understood as musical "poietics" as distinguished from mere practice). The incidental (a matter of performance practices) became essential (a particle of the composition). Anything incidental, because improvised, leans toward formularization, toward subjection to simple and fixed rules and models. Improvisation is always tied to models; otherwise it would quickly stagnate or go astray.

Judged from the standpoint of the integrated work, the connection of the incidental and improvised with the other elements of composition or performance is exposed to an unfortunate alternative between convention and arbitrariness. Contrasts of piano and forte, as long as they are not notated, either turn into a rigidly mechanical echo mannerism attached to each repetition or they get scattered over a piece following the accidental mood of the moment as effects to titillate the listener. Dynamics, specific without being mannered in the bad sense of the word (an example of mannered dynamics intended as a model for improvisation is given by Quantz in his *Versuch*), became possible only when integrated in the composition as a part of which the diverse relations to melody, rhythm, and harmony are ingredients of a compositional calculation directed toward the form as a whole.

Differentiation, which in the biological model appears as a premise or complement of integration, would be insufficiently described by a bare reference to a wealth of musical distinctions without considering the kinds of distinction, which are of unequal aesthetic relevance.

1. A superficial but by no means useless criterion is the material differentiation, that is, the affluence of a musical vocabulary in regard to rhythmic figures, harmonies, dissonances, and melodic groupings. While inadequate for the foundation of an aesthetic judgment, it does not deserve to be underestimated. The disdain in which it is sometimes held becomes double talk or aesthetic counterfeit when references to the irrelevance of material differentiation serve to justify triviality, as if platitudes were the protector of noble simplicity. It is precisely against trumped-up primitivism, which claims that complications mean nothing, that differentiation, even the merely material one, resumes the impor-

tance of a valid aesthetic criterion which it generally lacks. The abuse of the criterion is in any case less offensive than the abuse of skepticism toward the criterion.

2. Functional differentiation is aesthetically more relevant than material differentiation; for, metaphorically speaking, it widens not the musical vocabulary but the syntax. Functional differentiation appears not always as a consequence, but sometimes as the opposite, of material differentiation. In that case, shrinkage of the one becomes the premise for growth of the other. In tonal harmony of the seventeenth century, the result of a selection, the inventory of available chord connections was smaller than in the modal technique of the sixteenth century, which admitted excessive chromatization of chords because alteration did not disturb their feebly stamped cohesion. (When E-minor and C-major chords merely stand next to each other without the one tending to the other of which it is a function, one can without contradiction change E minor chromatically to E major, and C major to C minor. Carlo Gesualdo's chromaticism, apparently a licentiousness, is actually the strict, if also extreme, consequence of a harmony that does not subordinate but juxtaposes.) The material reduction of harmonies in the seventeenth century is the reverse of functional differentiation. Chords now appear as parts of a comprehensive system of functions or wide network of immediate and indirect relations. They no longer lie next to each other without further obligation or, at best, like links of a chain, committed exclusively only to the preceding and the following chords.

Aesthetically and historically, tonal harmony does not stand on a higher step than modality: the systems belong to different periods. Functionalism provides, if at all, a negative criterion: a functional analysis prevents the error of considering the selective harmony of the seventeenth century an impoverishment and regression.

Although unusual, the term "functional form", in analogy to functional harmony, need not sound strange. In many musical works, the sections fulfill differentiated functions, although evidently not all musical forms are functional unless one insists on designating beginning, middle, and end as functions.

In order not to fall apart or to appear as a mere succession (which does not conclude but just stops), a musical form extending across hundreds of measures must form a system of functions. Differentiation is here the prerequisite of integration. Only when the sections of a movement—introduction and theme, areas of unfolding and resolution, transitions and closing groups, development and recapitulation—stand out clearly against one another do they join so closely together as to create a "big form," which at the same time spans a wide arch and is readily perceivable. It is not the variety of themes and motives but the wealth of characteristic melodies and rhythms which unmistakably stamp a definite formal function.

3. From material and functional differentiation one must separate—if the neologism be permitted—a relational one which proceeds, not from any single element of the composition (harmony, rhythm, dynamics), but from relationships between elements. The contrast, for instance, between counterpoint of the *seconda pratica* of the seventeenth century and that of the *prima pratica*, derives largely from the changed relationship between dissonance and rhythm or meter: passing dissonances were moved from a weak to a strong beat; and syncopated dissonances, conversely, from a strong to a weak beat. The dissonances—the *transitus inversus* and the *syncopatio inversa*, as Christoph Bernhard called them—are thus new neither in a material sense as technical phenomena nor in a functional sense but in a strictly relational sense: as the result of an altered position in the measure of a technically customary feature.

The aesthetic relevance, to be sure, is minimal. Relational differentiation is closer to material than to functional differentiation.

Principles of form

The schemata of the doctrine of musical forms, as drafted in the early nineteenth century by Adolf Bernhard Marx, are in disrepute as empty shells. Originally, however, the doctrine of forms, the work of an enthusiast and not of a pedant, was intended as phenomenology in Hegel's sense, as a description of phenomenalized forms of the spirit realizing itself. In the principles of sonata form and fugue, Marx, the Hegelian among music theorists, saw, as it were, the substance of music history. The individual work

appeared as the sample of a formal type, as the partial and one-
sided realization of a formal idea fully and comprehensively
realized only by the whole history of a form. Not just the work but
the form, the generality, represented a piece of musical life.

Whereas Marx acknowledged the Platonism of his music
theory, convinced of the reality of the idea, most analysts of the last
decades have been nominalists. Where Marx looked for form ideas,
they see nothing but schemata serving not a normative but merely a
heuristic function. Insofar as the schemata are not entirely dis-
dained, they are used as if they were experimental instructions; the
goal of analysis is not the presentation of a work in relation to the
idea of a form—the idea of sonata or fugue—but the cancellation of
the general schema through the description of the individual case.
The concepts underlying an analysis do not express the essence of a
work but are a detour, even if unavoidable and "methodical,"
toward the contemplation and description of the individual.

The divergent convictions, the contrast between Platonism
and nominalism in music theory, is important not only to the
history of musical thinking but also to the judgment about the
musical works themselves. The general concept or ideal type of a
musical form (sonata or fugue), which gradually faded to a schema in
the late nineteenth century and eventually degenerated to a label,
still possessed historical substance around 1800. It was musically
real. Therefore the fulfillment of the postulates contained in the
idea of a form was a valid aesthetic criterion. The aesthetic and
technical irrelevance of the musical doctrine of forms around 1900
does not prove that it was always irrelevant.

The aesthetic significance of forms and ideas of forms—not
only of single forms but of form in general—is, on the one hand,
subject to historic changes (being doubtless smaller in the twentieth
century than around 1800). One may wonder, on the other hand,
whether ideas of form in various periods and realms of music (of the
sixteenth and seventeenth centuries, for example, or of the salon
and chamber music of the nineteenth century) admit aesthetic
comparisons that are not idle speculations. One of the topics dear to
historians afraid to lose their way in the labyrinths of aesthetics—let
alone aesthetics permeated by historic-philosophic reflections—is
the maxim that the desire to establish a rank order of ideas of form

and of works belonging to different periods or heterogeneous traditions is nonsense. The thesis, however, that the aesthetic rank of all periods is in principle the same, or ought to be considered the same out of historic justice, is no less speculative than the disreputable antithesis that it is not the same. A rigorous empiricist can actually only say that he knows nothing about the "immediacy to God" of each period—according to Ranke's seemingly innocuous, but truly confounded theological dictum—and that one must not exclude the possibility that *sub specie aeternitatis* some periods appear aesthetically significant and others miserable.

Thus it remains unsettled whether in a comparison across time barriers the appraisal of functionally more differentiated music as also the aesthetically richer is sensible or untenable. Within one period, however, and under equal or similar stylistic and technical conditions, the validity of such an appraisal need not be doubted. It can be challenged on the grounds that the concept of stylistic and technical conditions is too vague and intangible. In order to draw the borders within which the contrast between functionally differentiated and nondifferentiated forms offers a solid aesthetic criterion, one must isolate form principles characteristic of different periods or traditions and not reducible one to the other.

1. The concept of a continuous series is exposed to the suspicion of being a simplistic solution or a terminological mask for a defective mode of musical form. The absence of connections and developments, the juxtaposition of musically self-sufficient moments that neither derive from the preceding nor prepare the following, is diametrically opposed to the idea of form in a musical doctrine proposing a relation of the parts to each other and to the whole. Form analysis would not know where to begin.

Yet one is reluctant to speak of the decline of form in view of the keyboard music of the early eighteenth century, characterized by contemporaries as "gallant" (a term indistinctly comprising both a stylistic concept and a fashionable word). The pathetic verdict ends in a void; "gallant" music, while appearing patchy to the form analyst, is not without inner cohesion. The unity derives less from themes and motives than from style and manner. The adherence of these piece, which one can hardly call works, to a definite "tone," a musical "conversational tone," suffices to view the loose fitting of phrases and sections not as a crumbling form but rather as an attitude appropriate to a musical conversation in which erudite language would be excessive. Musical "labor" and a "learned" instead of a "gallant" pose would appear as offenses against the "conversational tone," as pedantry betraying poor taste and aesthetic insensitivity.

The principle of a continuous series was historically endangered because its aesthetic *raison d'être* consisted of the unity and equanimity of a "gallant conversational tone." In a style defined by contrasts, it lost the aesthetic hold it had enjoyed in the early eighteenth century. As the degenerate form of the principle of a continuous series, there arises the potpourri, the formal prototype of nineteenth-century trivial music. In the potpourri, the stylistic unity of the conversational piece is replaced by provocative variegation, by a piling-up of heterogeneous sections which do not form real contrasts—contrast is a principle of form concentration— but only clash glaringly with each other. The series becomes an aesthetic flaw through heterogeneity, and also the other way around. (In some movements by Mahler, heterogeneous elements are indeed gathered, but they are drawn into the developmental process of the form which rescues them from the potpourri triviality to which they would succumb if treated *seriatim.*)

2. Musical form based on mere juxtaposition of sections arouses distrust leading to exaggerated criticism—form analysts tend to interpret the inappropriateness of their method as a deficiency of the object. Yet the spinning-out type as represented by the works of Bach and Vivaldi enjoys a historic-aesthetic prestige which may be challenged insofar as it includes various misunderstandings. One does an aesthetic injustice to the music of the late baroque, which one admires, by reacting only to the irresistible drive (associated with the word "spinning-out") which one can enjoy without thinking. (The misunderstanding becomes in no way legitimized by the intrusion of "motorism" into compositional practice during the 1920s: the results were meager.) With Bach— and in the more important works of Vivaldi—this drive, although very effective, is not the aesthetically decisive factor. Rather, it forms the background against which the differentiations of the

relevant details stand out in relief. Attempts to endow the regular, firm movement of the music represented by the *basso continuo* with ontologic importance and dignity are erroneous insofar as they rely upon a secondary element whose misuse as a primary element produces a false impression of the compositional technique.

3. The theory of musical form is pervaded by a tendency toward dualistic typologies which meet the desire for simple antitheses but also distort the more complicated historic reality. Even in the music of the eighteenth and nineteenth centuries, the main focus of the theory of musical forms, at least four principles must be distinguished: besides the principles of a continuous series and of spinning-out, those of developing and grouping.

The development principle, of which the outer compositional skin is created by thematic and motivic working-out, has been investigated and characterized so often that a recapitulating description would be superfluous pedantry. Movements built according to the development principle are the primary and historically determined objects of an analysis of forms aimed at revealing motivic relationships that give a composition inner cohesion.

4. The principle of grouping, however, has barely been recognized as an independent form idea or been adequately analyzed, although the simple song forms, which usually provide the starting point for instruction in musical form, are based on groupings. Two constitutive elements collaborate: the recurrence of melodic sections which need not have the character and function of themes or motives (Hugo Riemann's identification of "thematic" with "recurring" was an error with far-reaching consequences), and the regularity of periodicity—the "squaring of compositional construction," as Wagner sneeringly called it when he no longer needed it.

These two elements, which converge in song forms, are nevertheless independent of each other. Regular periodicity suffices—without melodic repetitions and recapitulations—to make a work cohesive and give it a backbone (paradigmatic are long stretches in Wagner's *Lohengrin* which are melodically new at every instant and rhythmically consistently "square"). Conversely, in works in which melodic elements or motives steadily recur, periodicity can resolve into "rhythmic prose" without endangering intelligibility (in regard to formal technique, the *Ring* tetralogy is the opposite of *Lohengrin*). Forms built by groupings that rely on recurring motives rather than on periodicity tend to become developmental.

Analogy and compensation

The technique of composition includes—unintentionally rather than purposefully—a calculation of the aesthetic effect. At all times the tendency to balance complexity in one direction by simplicity in another seems to have prevailed. The simple and customary—invariable meter or limited chord vocabulary—provided the support and foil for complications in rhythmic or motivic details or in harmonic-tonal relationships.

Carlo Gesualdo's chromaticism, a document of the provocatively excessive mannerism around 1600, was restricted to sections within a simple homophonic texture almost free of dissonances. In more differentiated polyphony with complex dissonant figures, Gesualdo strictly avoided chromaticism.

In the eighteenth and nineteenth centuries, the preservation of the same meter within a symphonic movement, even across hundreds of measures, was a compositional norm never violated, as though it were a law of nature. It became such a fixed habit and proposition of musical hearing that one is hardly struck by the oddity that a work of such complex inner structure as the first movement of the "Eroica" fits into the simple scheme of a 3/4 meter. Rather than balancing each other, the complexity of the thematic-motivic development and the simplicity of the meter almost produce a contradiction endangering the aesthetic cohesion of the piece.

In the *Fantastic Symphony,* style and form pull in opposite directions. As Schumann already recognized with surprise, the anticlassicist Berlioz, whose music in the history of composition marks the strongest imaginable break with tradition, kept himself in regard to form within the bounds of a symphonic movement with thematic contrast, development, and recapitulation. For all his revolutionary spirit, he wished to be understood by the public.

While thin fragmentary texture and prevalence of slow hesitating tempi are doubtless founded in the nature of a composer like Webern, they also appear as compensation and counterpart to the labyrinthic involutions with which Webern experimented in the system of tonal relations. And it is no accident that through Webern, not Schönberg, dodecaphony in recent decades achieved a fame which—paradoxically stated—weaves together popular and esoteric features. Webern's music, although seemingly inaccessible and introvert, is "more easily understandable" than Schönberg's.

If not the composers themselves who tried to balance the simple against the complex, it was the public which neglected one of the elements of the piece in order to focus on another. To do justice to Bach's polyphony and harmony at the same time and without slighting one or the other aspect seems almost impossible. At the various stages of Bach reception, different features were thus emphasized as primary and decisive, not without connection to the compositional tendencies of a period: around 1900, harmony; two decades later, "linear counterpoint." Because one refused to confess one's own incapacity to hear adequately both phases at the same time, the inclination was very strong to regard the element standing in the shade as secondary and dependent—polyphony as "unfolded" harmony or inversely harmony as the "result" or even the "by-product" of counterpoint. Offense against the principle of compensation—and Bach's work clearly challenges the idea of economy by proving its uncertainty or at least restricting its validity—creates aesthetic embarrassment.

Arnold Schönberg indeed recognized the principle of compensation or economy as a fact of musical hearing and as a historically effective tendency, but he repudiated it as a critical authority of aesthetics. Schönberg, who regarded the middle road ("the only one that does not lead to Rome") as suspect and contemptible, thought in rigorous and anticlassicistic terms. His antithesis to the principle of compensation—the assertion that music must be equally developed in all dimensions in order to be attuned—was based on the undeniable fact that each element of the composition—melody, counterpoint, harmony, and rhythm—is closely and inseparably tied to all others and becomes what it is only through the manifold relationships in which it participates. In Wagner's music no less than Bach's, richer polyphony produces more intricate harmony; complications of rhythm, which is an integral part of melody, cannot be without influence on the pitch arrangement if disturbing divergences are to be avoided. "This is why," Schönberg writes in *Style and Idea,* "when composers have acquired the technique of filling one direction with content to the utmost capacity, they must do the same in the next direction, and finally in all the directions in which music expands."[1]

The idea of a music in which all elements are analogously developed and cooperate with equal right sounds utopian. The objection suggests itself that in dodecaphony, Schönberg's own technique, the elaboration of harmony stayed behind that of counterpoint; yet wanting to refute an idea on the grounds that it cannot be totally realized is a sign of embarrassment and rancor. (Schönberg's postulate places compositional technique and dodecaphonic aesthetics in a paradoxical relationship to each other. Simultaneous dodecaphonic penetration of melody and harmony, voice leading and concord, succeeds smoothly in the simple schematized type of "melody with chordal support." It becomes increasingly difficult, however, the more closely the texture—through richer polyphony leading to more complex chord structures—approaches Schönberg's idea of equal development "in all directions.")

Both Stravinsky and Schönberg have been reproached—for opposite reasons—for unequal development of melody and rhythm. Denial of the fact would be a false and weak apology. One may wonder whether the inequality, which is evident, signifies a technical-aesthetic disproportion and whether thus the principles of compensation or analogy possess the authority to decide. Do Stravinsky's rudimentary melodies, shriveled to formulas or broken into fragments, contradict his complicated rhythms, or are they, precisely because of their simplicity, their support and complementation? And is the divergence between Schönberg's dodecaphonic atonal melodies and his rhythms, which derive from the propositions of the tonal period, a technical-aesthetic deficiency, or is it

---

1. The English of the quotation is Schönberg's.

rather the condition for the realization by both dodecaphony and the given rhythms of the function aimed at by Schönberg, namely, to be constituent elements of the "big form" to which Schönberg always felt himself attracted? To function and be recognizable as themes, the rhythmic characters had to lean on tradition. If one proceeds from the form as a whole—and not, like the serialists who reproached Schönberg for composing incongruously, from technical details—the divergence between rhythm and melody in works like the Third and Fourth String Quartets by Schönberg appears as a dialectic contradiction.

As Schönberg's own practice as a composer shows, the principle of analogy is thus subject to restrictions. What from one point of view—technique of composition—appears as disagreement between melody and rhythm, from the other point of view—form—may constitute a necessity. Nevertheless, the agreement of richly differentiated as well as analogously developed elements of a piece of music, as postulated by Schönberg in *Style and Idea,* is one of the criteria from which the attempt may proceed to sustain and justify aesthetic through factual judgments, even if more precise analysis compels one to make some modifications. The principle of compensation or economy, the opposite authority to the principle of analogy, explains the intelligibility and success of musical works rather than their rank. The compensation principle is an exoteric criterion; the analogy principle is an esoteric criterion.

Audibility

The commonplace that music must be heard and understood through hearing if it is not to become a pale shadow of itself seems obvious and banal, but it is not self-evident. In any case, it has been so obstinately and emphatically repeated that one wonders whether its validity is endangered. The suspicion arises that audible music is becoming overgrown by "paper music" whose structure is visible in the notation without becoming acoustically phenomenalized; it is becoming distorted by analytic methods which cling to the text instead of proceeding from the musical experience. One is almost made to believe that notation in music is an evil. The most frequent topic in the criticism of new music is the reproach that precisely the elements believed to form the substance of the composed piece remain inaudible. The reproach is based on the premise that anything merely thought through but not audibly realized has no aesthetic validity. Yet the criterion of audibility, in the crude version in which it circulates, is thoroughly questionable.

1. The aesthetic disdain of "superfluous intentions" not "realized" in the perceptible shape of a work originated in the polemics of classicism against mannered and baroque art. The symbol whose significance is brought out fully in appearance was praised; the allegory was rejected. Although the tendency toward "paper music"—unintelligible without perusal and analysis of the notated text—must not be compared to allegorical inclinations, an undogmatic theory of art must recognize that the criterion of audibility, of complete realization by perception, is not a natural law of aesthetics but a postulate of historically limited scope. By rigorously restricting the concept of music or of "music proper" to the perceptible, one curtails historic reality for the sake of a dogma not older than the eighteenth century.

2. The opinion that music loses its aesthetic right to exist when it has to be read is motivated socially rather than factually. It originated, not as a reflection of the development of composition in the eighteenth and nineteenth centuries, but as a justification of musical illiteracy based on the banal fact that musical notation, unlike written language, is socially useless outside art. One need not hope for propagation of musical literacy on the model of linguistic literacy. It would be an error to draw an analogy from literary to musical works—to imagine that the transition from poetry recited to poetry read could set the example for a similar transmutation of musical hearing into musical reading. The relation of the semantic to the acoustic element, of the significance to its carrier, is in principle not the same in language as in music. Yet it would be an exaggeration to legitimize aesthetically musical illiteracy and to deny that it represents an obstacle to adequate hearing. The aesthetic "immediacy" one tries to preserve by keeping notation away from laymen is a phantom. The seemingly ingenuous hearing of musical illiterates is in reality caught in the schemes of the entertainment industry; aesthetic freedom relating "immediately"

and free of dogmas to the object can hardly be achieved except by the detour of emancipation from the ingrained—an emancipation which employs the tool of reflection about music mediated by notation.

3. The alternative that an element of the composition be either audible or inaudible is too rigid and crude to be adequate. To keep concepts from hardening into slogans, one must distinguish degrees of audibility, not only psychologically or physiologically, but aesthetically. In every musical work, even the simplest, a foreground to be clearly perceived stands in relief against a background half lying in shadow. The blurring of outlines in a secondary layer of music is not a deficiency of musical hearing, not an incidental inadequacy of the ear, but a feature belonging to the aesthetic essence of the piece. Vagueness and intangibility may even determine the comprehensive character of an entire work, not only of a single layer. Anyone trying to apperceive every detail in Wagner's "Magic Fire Music" or in many pieces by Debussy hears aesthetically incorrectly. Exactness is inadequate.

The opinion, on the other hand, that the structure of a work has to be apperceived consciously in order to be effective is a prejudice in need of limitation lest it lead to errors. Not only affective but also logical elements can be apprehended half-consciously. One does not have to penetrate a syllogism to experience the cogency of a deduction; and a hearer of dodecaphonic music feels the density of the nexus without conscious awareness of the system of tonal relations. Nobody is so dull as to misinterpret twelve-tone music, with all its external ruggedness, as an improvisation. The impression of strictness and logic prevails, even if one does not know the premises.

4. Reading a text in musical notation is always accompanied by acoustical imagination, which sometimes indeed remains shadowy. Conversely, musical hearing is permeated by elements that had been transmitted through writing. The separation of hearing and reading is abstract in a bad sense.

Paper music as painted in the polemics against serial composition—music that has cut the tie to audible phenomena—is a conceptual ghost; it has never existed. Even the most recondite canonic structures always stayed within the borders of the tonal system and the consonance-dissonance order drawn for the music of a given period. They did not—as one might expect if constructive, pseudo-mathematical interests had really cut themselves loose from music, using tones as mere ciphers of a code—advance into abstract realms beyond the reach of accoustical imagination. Paper music— one may retain the polemical term while pursuing apologetic designs—does not exist independently of acoustic-musical imagination but merely diminishes the role of hearing in favor of relational thinking.

5. The divergence between, on the one hand, a compositional practice whose results are not intelligible without analytic reading of the notated text and, on the other hand, a public consisting mainly of musical illiterates (a condition of which it is neither ashamed nor need be ashamed) is profound but need not indicate a separation. In contrast to linguistic structures, music can be effective without being understood. (The category of "understanding" is problematic in music aesthetics.) The history of musical hearing, which nobody knows, may even be independent of the history of composition to a degree that clouds the concept of a development "of music" in which composition and reception interact. Without exaggeration, one may claim that the aesthetic rift—the dichotomy between a structure which nobody discerns without laborious analysis and an acoustical façade which nevertheless makes its effect—is a character trait and indeed a constituent of new music. Modern compositions appear simultaneously as paper music and "effect" music.

Analyses

Bach: Cantata 106 (*Actus tragicus*)

Next to Cantata 21, "Ich hatte viel Bekümmernis," Bach's Cantata 106, "Gottes Zeit ist die allerbeste Zeit," was one of the few vocal works which the nineteenth century—a period that, while praising Bach as *Erzkantor* ("archicantor"), saw him primarily as a composer of instrumental music—accepted without resistance. One of the reasons was doubtless that the text of the *Actus tragicus* consists mainly of Bible quotations instead of "madrigalesque poetry," whose "baroque bombast", the mixture of dialectics and extravagance, was felt to be unbearable as long as the aesthetic sentiment was stamped by classicism.

In his criticism of the *Actus tragicus*, Moritz Hauptmann, cantor at St. Thomas's, was nevertheless of two minds. "What a wonderful inwardness," he wrote to Otto Jahn (overlooking the rhetorical character of the musical text representation which leans on traditional topoi). "No measure that is conventional, everything is thoroughly felt. Among the cantatas I know there is none in which all and everything is so firm and appropriate to musical significance and expression." The enthusiasm is, however, broken by reflection, the sentimental aesthetics by formalism. "If one wanted to and could suspend one's feelings for this kind of beauty and look at the whole as a piece of musical architecture, then it becomes a curious monster of movements shoved on top of, and grown into, each other, just like the similarly patched-together phrases of the text, without any orderly grouping or climax." Philipp Spitta, quoting

Hauptmann's criticism in his Bach biography, appropriated the praise as "well-grounded" and rejected the censure as "unfounded." Yet the part Spitta mistook is the complementation and reverse image of the other. The character of the *Actus tragicus,* the concentrated expressiveness and rhetoric, cannot be separated from the form which gives the effect of a patchwork. Regular musical architecture, missed in the cantata by Hauptmann, is inconceivable if one insists that "no measure be conventional." A musical work with the aim and idea of spanning a wide arch and yet being readily comprehensible is never one in which "everything is thoroughly felt."

The reproach of "formlessness" raised by Hauptmann may be assailable if one is concerned with historic justice, but it is technically and aesthetically not so "unfounded" as Spitta believed it to be in his apologetic zeal. The *Actus tragicus* was written before 1714, probably in 1707 or 1708, in Mühlhausen and still represents the "older cantata type" which should properly not be called cantata but spiritual concerto. (For aesthetic judgment, the name of the type is irrelevant.) The various sections, ariosi rather than arias, have not yet completely congealed into independent, closed movements. A feeling for form that expects unambiguity will be disappointed: whether the alto arioso "In deine Hände" stands by itself (it differs tonally from what follows) or acts as the first part of a duet remains undecided. Compared to the type of "large form" developed in Italy around 1700, the forms in the *Actus tragicus* are unfinished and rudimentary. The da capo aria with a differentiated ritornello which supplies the thematic framework and backbone of a movement was utilized by Bach only in the Weimar cantatas after 1714.

Although a musical conservative, Spitta judged in the spirit of his time—a period which regarded "musical architecture," as Hauptmann called it, as secondary and felt itself attracted to an expressiveness and rhetoric which broke through conventions of musical form, seeing in the deviation from the norm a means toward emphatic, drastic expression. The patchwork of the *Actus tragicus* was perceived in the nineteenth century—without clear articulation of the aesthetic premises—not as a deficiency but as a real merit, a suspension of formal conventionalities for the sake of expressiveness. Around 1710, however, the closed and at the same time widely arched and readily comprehensible form was not a hollow convention to be relinquished but, on the contrary, a goal toward which the development of composing aspired insofar as it did not remain stubbornly provincial. The fame of the *Actus tragicus* in the nineteenth century—if our reconstruction of aesthetic premises is valid—thus rested on an inversion of the historic situation. The patched or broken form, archaic in the early eighteenth century, looked modern in the nineteenth; and the closed large form, for which Bach in 1714 reached because it was new, appeared in retrospect as an inhibiting convention.

The procedure of measuring forms pieced together of divergent parts ("monsters" according to Hauptmann) by a formal type extending without break in continuity over hundreds of measures may be criticized for reaching a slanted comparison by squeezing together heterogeneous elements belonging to different traditions. This objection seems all the more valid if one perceives and classifies the "older cantata type" as a spiritual concerto, a genre in its own right, and not a rudimentary antecedent of the newer cantata consisting of recitatives and arias.

The *Actus tragicus* is a work of transition, not only historically—as a form whose propositions and consequences reach into two periods—but also in an aesthetic and technical sense. It is marked by ambivalences and indecisiveness. Without becoming suspect of teleological inclinations which turn the labyrinth of history into a one-way street, one can readily discern in a movement like the bass aria "Bestelle dein Haus" a preliminary form of the cantata aria— an undeveloped disposition toward the large form spun out of one theme.

This aria is an arioso insofar as it is tonally not closed but—as part of a complex of movements "grown into each other," as Hauptmann put it—mediates between C minor and F minor. Syntactically, on the other hand, it contains the seeds for a far-reaching development. The theme manifests the so-called "spinning-out" type with a motto-like antecedent, a spun-out continuation in sequences, and a cadential epilogue (mm. 5-13). The two following sections, consisting of sequences based on fragments of the theme, appear as the second stage of spinning-out (mm. 18-40). The syntax of the theme supplies the model for the organization of the overall form: the relation of antecedent to spinning-out returns in augmentation in the relation of theme to development or continuation.

The tendency toward a large form is noticeable without, however, realizing and establishing itself. In this regard, the cantata is the work of a transition period. Instead of setting a complementary middle section against the main section, the aria breaks off with a return of the first two measures of the theme—a reminiscence rather than a recapitulation—and an instrumental postlude. (The formal effect of fragmentation is not without significance for the musical interpretation of the text: the abrupt character of the end underscores the threat of the words *Bestelle dein Haus* ("Set thine house in order: for thou shalt die, and not live." Isaiah 38:1) with which Isaiah admonished King Hezekiah.

The aria shrinks to an arioso. The absence of a middle section is not a matter of chance but a deficiency explainable in terms of historic style. In order not to dissolve and turn indistinct because of the expansion a middle section would produce—the large form of the early eighteenth century is an architectural form with firm outlines—the movement would have to be held and clamped together by the recurring thematic scaffolding of an instrumental ritornello. But the creation of an instrumental ritornello in "Bestelle dein Haus" was blocked by an obviously vocal melodic invention, determined by details of the text to such an extent as to prove unintelligible in an instrumental version or paraphrase.

The form of the aria "Bestelle dein Haus" is hence ambiguous. Interlocked in contradiction are old and new; the melodic vocabulary of the spiritual concerto and the syntax of the cantata aria; restraint within the tight form clinging to the text and a half-suppressed tendency toward a broad form emancipated from the details of the text. Insofar as the *Actus tragicus* no longer represents intact the "older cantata type" to the tradition of which it belongs, criticism of its form proceeding from the "tendency" instead of the "derivation" of the work is not so unfounded and illegitimate as it may appear to a rigorous historian for whom every moment of history is "immediate to God."

Johann Stamitz: Symphony in D major

The symphony in D major by Johann Stamitz (*Denkmäler der Tonkunst in Bayern* III/1, p.14) was the opening piece of *Melodia Germanica,* a representative collection of Mannheim symphonies printed in Paris before 1760. The work was esteemed as a paradigm of the "new music" of the eighteenth century which its contemporaries considered equally fascinating and perplexing.

Hugo Riemann, who discovered (or constructed) the historic importance of Stamitz—not without exaggerated accentuation—investigated the works from the viewpoint of historical development. The level which they represented in the history of the genre (symphonic sonata form) seemed decisive to him; the criterion he leaned on was the extent to which the second contrasting subject, the thematic-motivic workmanship, and the recapitulation of the main theme were clearly present. In the case of Riemann, the aesthetic judgment can hardly be separated from the historic. To a historian convinced that the development of a musical form strives toward classicism in which it achieves perfection by completely realizing its idea, the historic distance from classicism necessarily appears as an aesthetic one. The archaic is downgraded to a preliminary step, mannerism to a form of decadence.

The method centered on historic development which treats a musical creation, to put it emphatically, not as a work but as a document—witness of a historic situation—was rejected with polemic vehemence by Werner Korte ("Darstellung eines Satzes von Johann Stamitz," *Festschrift für Karl Gustav Fellerer,* 1962). Korte, inclined toward a variant of structuralism, tried to determine a composer's individual law of form. He named the principle he discovered in the symphonies by Stamitz *Streuungsverfahren* ("process of scattering"). To distinguish Stamitz's characteristic disposition of a movement from Haydn's and Beethoven's, he spoke of a "kaleidoscopical scattering of thematic units," as if the sections were arbitrarily interchangeable.

The term "process of scattering" is meant to be strictly descriptive; it implies no aesthetic judgment. Yet one cannot easily push aside the familiar view that a structure whose parts are arbitrarily interchangeable occupies a lower step in the hierarchy of forms than a genre in which richer functional differentiation and firmer, tighter integration of sections mutually complement and condition each other. Is the "process of scattering" a principle of form in its own right, asserting itself irreducibly and aesthetically incontestably along with the principles of development and of grouping?

Korte's presentation of Stamitz's procedure tends, for the sake of polemics, to distortions. Its main weakness is the contradiction between references, on the one hand, to a "dice principle" (accidental transpositions) and, on the other hand, to functional differentiation of sections, although the one strictly speaking excludes the other. When a period has the character of an "opening theme," it cannot—unless crucially modified—occupy a closing position without aesthetic damage produced by the "process of scattering."

The contradiction can be resolved. The reconciliation between differentiation and interchangeability—both elements are clearly present—is accomplished by a process of grouping ignored or neglected by Korte. The first movement of the D-major symphony is organized into seven groups each comprising two or three sections:

Groups	I	II	III	IV	V	VI	VII
Sections	*a b c*	*d e*	*f g*	*b d h*	*d c e*	*f b g*	*b g*
Measures	8 8 8	7 6	12 8	12 6 6	9 6 6	12 8 4	4 7

Sections *a*, *d*, and *f* are unmistakably beginnings. Melodically and dynamically—by their thematic memorability and dynamic tendency toward piano—they stand out distinctly against the nonthematic sections which form either a crescendo transition or a forte contrast. Section *b* is a "Mannheim Walze" (crescendo passage), *e* is a spinning-out sequence with cadence; *c* and *g* manifest themselves as culminations or, maliciously described, as noisy tutti, experienced by Schubart as "cataracts."

In groups I-III the order of the sections is patently founded on their functional differentiation. In the recapitulation, on the other hand, in groups V-VII, the sections are displaced in a seemingly confused and arbitrary manner, so that the notion of a "dice principle" intrudes. Yet the appearance of being accidental and unfounded is an illusion. The principles can be reconstructed, and the exceptions are not unmotivated.

1. Sections *a, d,* and *f* always stand at the beginning of a group: after a caesura preceded by a cadence. The other sections are interlocked. One exception is the crescendo transition *b* in groups IV and VII. In group IV—the description implies indeed an aesthetic judgment—it occurs, irregularly and functionally reduced, between two cadences (theme *d* enters regularly after a caesura). In group VII its fusion with the characteristic motive from theme *f* renders it quasi-thematic.

2. If one accepts the principle that periods, while functionally characterized as beginnings, transitions, and endings, may be used so that one beginning or transition may be substituted for another without making the grouping unintelligible, then the substitution of *d* for theme *a* in the recapitulation (group V) is formally quite as justified as the displacement of *b* from group I (between *a* and *c*) into group VI (between *f* and *g*). Section *b,* the "Mannheim Walze," is simply a transition, not a specific mediation between *a* and *c.* The functional differentiation is general, not individual.

3. Functionally, *b* is a transition, and *c* is an ending. Their assumption of other positions (*b* in IV, the development, is the opening section; *c* in V is the middle section) is not founded on the form principle of the movement, on the arbitrariness of the "process of scattering," but rather rests upon an added "artful device": the plagal cadence which characterizes *c* in I as an ending is missing in V but appended in IV to *b* so that the opening theme *d* is regularly preceded by a caesura.

The sections become interchangeable—contrary to their original functional positioning—by means of the primitive but characteristic "artful device" of adding or omitting the cadential formula. If one tries to reconstruct the genesis of symphonic form in the works of Stamitz, the usual conception, oriented by the model of an organism, according to which interchangeability of sections signifies a rudimentary early condition, and functional differentiation a higher later degree of development, fails us. For Stamitz obviously presupposes—there is no other explanation for his "artful device"—functional differentiation, that is, the characterization of sections as beginning, middle, and end of a group; and he resorts to interchangeability only secondarily in the belief that the variety of the unexpected is needed in order to appear interesting at every instant. If one admits functional differentiation and integration of the differentiated items as a classical norm, the idea of form realized by Stamitz is not so much archaic as mannered.

The outlines of sonata form, though denied by Korte, are evident. Main theme is *a*, second subject is *f*. (Already *d* is in the dominant but sounds like a variant of *a* rather than a second subject; as occasionally in sonata forms by Hadyn, the two characteristics of a second subject — the melodic and the tonal — do not coincide.) Group IV is a modulating development with sequences of the split-off opening measures of *d*. In the recapitulation (V to VII), theme *a* changes places with the variant *d;* but as a kind of reminiscence and intimation of the modified formal function, the two opening measures of *a* precede the return of *d*.

Insofar as sonata form presupposes functional differentiation of the sections, it is imperiled by the tendency toward interchangeability. But it is not so much "underdeveloped" — thus the objection against the design based on historic development could be formulated — as rather secondarily "distorted." Out of the historic judgment, one reaches an aesthetic one: for the sake of checkered variety, Stamitz negates the functional differentiation of the sections which he has only half accomplished and which completely realized would suffice to avoid the monotony that Stamitz deflects through mannerism.

Haydn: String Quartet in C major, opus 20 no. 2

Classicism is a double concept which comprises and inseparably interlocks historic and aesthetic elements. Firmly rooted is the thought that a musical work representing classicism must therefore be classical, although historians who shun aesthetic judgments tend to reduce the category "classicism" to a concept of periods and styles, which says nothing about the rank of the works it embraces. While the association of works by minor composers of the seventeenth century with the musical baroque seems harmless—if one does not altogether disdain such labels— even confirmed historians have difficulties counting Pleyel or Krommer, contemporaries and epigones of classicism, among the classics.

Ever since Adolf Sandberger decades ago in his essay "Zur Geschichte des Haydnschen Streichquartetts" (*Ausgewählte Aufsätze zur Musikgeschichte,* 1921, p. 224) designated the aesthetic-technical difference between opus 20 and opus 33 as a qualitative jump, historians have tenaciously agreed that Haydn's string quartets opus 33 make sensible the break between musical classicism and pre-classicism—a pre-classicism of which the more specific characterization as rococo, *Empfindsamkeit,* or *Sturm und Drang* has caused confusion rather than clarity in music history. The almost simultaneous creation with opus 33 of Goethe's *Iphigenie auf Tauris,* around 1780, may have aided the impression of a caesura in music history, of a transition to classicism, notwithstanding the vagueness and intangibility of the idea of a *Zeitgeist* ("a spirit of the times").

Sandberger explained the thematic-motivic working-out, which he saw as the new and characteristic features of the quartets opus 33, as the resolution of a contradiction Haydn encountered in opus 20: the contradiction between divertimento attitude and strict counterpoint. Three of the six quartets in opus 20 end with a fugue or fugato finale, although they also show traces of their origin in the "lower style" (to use the language of North German aesthetics of the eighteenth century). It thus seems that Haydn had forced together heterogeneous and mutually exclusive traditions: the "gallant" and the "learned" styles. "With all his sensitive mediation," Sandberger writes (pp. 259 f.) without pursuing the "mediation" analytically, "Haydn here coupled two things which in his world of the quartet—which is not Beethoven's world—had stylistically very little in common. . . . Here cassation quartet, there solemn counterpoint, here the new airy element, there the most profound constituent of musical equipment—these contradictions had to be felt by Haydn. Invaluable is the proof that Haydn, having arrived at this juncture, decided to abandon quartet composition for a full ten years. These pieces still lacked what was needed; there remained in them something unsatisfactory, a puzzling something was missing. Hence the master put aside the entire genre. What was missing was mediation between strict and free musical creation. The child of the marriage of counterpoint and freedom is thematic working-out."

Sandberger's historic description — the reconstruction of a problematic compositional situation out of which thematic working-out arose as solution — contains an aesthetic judgment. As a historical antecedent to opus 33, as a work of "pre-classicism" in its twofold sense, opus 20 is technically ambiguous. One must ask, however, in which sense, on the one hand, the thematic-motivic working-out, whose origin reaches back to the seventeenth century if not to an earlier period, is still underdeveloped and "pre-classical" in opus 20 and, on the other hand, whether in a single quartet as a concrete structure — and not merely in the abstract opposition of the "gallant" and the "learned" — a fugue or fugato finale signifies a stylistic break entangling the work in an aesthetic-technical contradiction. Is fugal texture a foreign heterogeneous element which happens to get from the outside, as it were, into a quartet like opus 20 no. 2 without being grounded in its stylistic conception?

One cannot deny that thematic-motivic working-out — in the wider sense of the concept — is characteristic of the first movement of opus 20 no. 2. It marks the movement and holds it together. The first part of the development section (mm. 48-60) follows a sequential model rhythmically indebted to a partial motive of the main theme (mm. 1-2). The rhythmic connection, to be sure, is associative rather than constitutive, and it does not belong specifically to the development section: the closing section of the exposition (mm. 39-42) is also rhythmically dependent on the main theme. In the second part of the development section (mm. 61-80), fragments of the exposition are drawn into a modulatory process without drastic melodic modification. The development process — measured by the method prevalent since opus 33 — thus suffers from the flaw that techniques appearing as extremes stand in closest juxtaposition. Either the connection with the theme is restricted to a particle of the melody — the rhythm — or the theme is not so much elaborated as merely quoted. But only the missing mediation —

according to Sandberger's form criticism—would be thematic working-out in the narrower classical sense.

While the thematic-motivic working-out in the first movement thus gives the impression of incongruity, the fugue finale—the second element in Sandberger's reconstruction of the historically problematic position of the work—is by no means a "learned" appendix protruding from the style of the quartet. The connection of divertimento themes and fugue technique—considered contradictory by Sandberger—rather marks a tendency governing all movements, namely, the tendency to explore cleverly the contrast between the "tone" of the gallant style and the "technique" of the strict style without aiming at a reconciling "synthesis." The contrast appears as an attraction. One is tempted to utilize Schlegel's category of the "interesting" to characterize aesthetically the conception of the quartet. In opus 20 no. 2, a work in which "pre-classical" conditions exist in their own right, inner contradiction is not a deficiency deserving an aesthetic verdict but rather a stylistic principle.

The incongruity—to avoid a seemingly negative aesthetic criticism, one could also speak of ambiguity if this pompous word were not too conspicuous—reaches into the very theme of the first movement. The beginning, marked by a standard syncopated dissonance, makes an archaistic impression; the continuation, on the other hand, seems "trifling," to use a fashionable word of the eighteenth century. While the theme is typical for a sonata movement, its initial presentation, according to the scheme of subject-answer-subject (together with two obbligato counterpoints), is reminiscent of fugal technique in the *sonata da chiesa*, one of the forerunners of the string quartet.

The second movement, an adagio, appears as "music about music," an instrumental emulation, but not copy, of a vocal model or type. The first part (mm. 1-33) is a "scena" with an archaistic ritornello at beginning and end (on the harmonic foundation of a sequence in fifths, antiquated by around 1770). The second part, a *cantabile* (mm. 34-63), presents itself as a "cavatina"—the entire movement is a paradigm of the "rhetorical style." The "scena," to put it paradoxically, is a recitative without recitation. It is recitative insofar as the solo voice is interrupted by typical orchestral insertions of a *recitativo accompagnato* which remind one of opera and cantata. Yet the violin part does not imitate the inflection of spoken language but remains characteristically instrumental. Borrowing one of the basic antitheses of classical aesthetics, one can define the principle of the movement as *aemulatio* and not as *imitatio*. In its own idiom, the violin emulates recitative instead of copying it.

In the third movement, the "gallant" style represented by the minuet from its very origin and therefore expected by the hearer, is breached in a "learned" way. The trio reminds one—and the reminiscence is almost a quotation—of the harmonic model of the archaistic adagio ritornello. The melody of the main section, moreover, is subjected to rhythmic-metric experiments which cross the dance character of the movement. The first phrase is organized not "squarely" but irregularly into four-times-five measures. In the recapitulation of the beginning (mm. 29-56), as if it were an analysis set to music, some of the irregular metrical groups are restored to their regular "square" basic forms (mm. 34-39 = 6-10 without 10 but with two new measures added; mm. 45-48 = 16-20 without 18; the irregular "superfluous" measures of the first phrase are thus 10 and 18). The artifice appears as a game whose rules are revealed by Haydn at the end of the movement.

If one looks for a comprehensive formula to characterize opus 20 no. 2 as a whole—a formula doing justice not only to the reinterpreting instrumental emulation of a vocal model or type in the adagio movement but also to the rhythmic-metric oddity of the minuet and to the precarious coupling of divertimento melody and fugue technique in the finale—one can underline as a common trait the experimental combination of heterogeneous elements (the idea of experiment, like that of manner, would have to be understood in a nonclassical sense). The incongruity in the finale, the contradiction between "the airiest and the most profound constituents of musical equipment" that Sandberger saw resolved by the classic form of thematic-motivic working-out, is not a problem to be isolated (in a singular case it would be a sign of aesthetic frangibility or questionableness) but rather proves to be a particular realization of a general principle dominating all movements of the composition. The contradiction in the statement of a historic development that investigates the postulates of classical style reached in opus 33 may perhaps brand it as a preliminary stage; within a continuity, in the aesthetic context of opus 20 no. 2, it is in no way a deficiency requiring removal but a constitutive characteristic of the style. It is high time to outline an aesthetic in which the "pre-classical" does not stand in the shadow of classicism.

Schubert: Piano Sonata in C minor, opus posthumum

The C-minor sonata, created in September 1828, a few weeks before Schubert's death, is one of his last three piano sonatas. To speak of a "late style" marking the work would be erroneous or at least dubious. Not that Schubert's early death prevents any sensible talk of a "late style"—the concept is a category of inner, not outer, chronology. But the spontaneous associations with the term "late style"—a collision of precarious concern for conventions with equally precarious recklessness in insisting on the uniquely personal—would miss the true character of the C-minor sonata. The problems of the work, and there are problems in the truest sense, are of a different kind.

As a composer of instrumental music, Schubert, at least in the earlier sonatas, is like a musical writer of epics, convinced that he is expected to spread out a variegated wealth of details. Impatience, driving toward a goal and end, is foreign to him. One has to listen to him as to a story teller for whom deviations, episodes, and interruptions are not distractions or delays of the main event but rather the main event itself.

But in his last sonatas, the tone changes. Schumann believed that he heard in them a touch of acquiescence and resignation. The review he wrote in 1838 on the posthumous publication of the works betrays disappointment: "Be it as it may, these sonatas seem to me very different from the others, particularly because of a much greater simplicity of invention, a voluntary renunciation of brilliant novelty when he used to make such great demands of himself—a spinning-out of certain general musical thoughts instead of weaving, as in the past, new threads into each phrase." Schumann seems to be talking only of melodic imagination, in which he senses a decline. Nevertheless the attempt may not be futile to support or explain his criticism by an analysis which will undertake to reconstruct the formal thought, the inner history, as it were, of the creation of the work.

The first movement of the C-minor sonata is in itself ambiguous. Traits reminiscent of Beethoven are interwoven with Schubert's own without a completely successful integration. The obvious reminiscence of the theme of Beethoven's C-minor Variations at the beginning of the sonata is not an indifferent accident but a sign or gesture by which Schubert seems to reveal his goal: the decisiveness and comprehensiveness he admired in Beethoven's music.

To counter his inclination toward digressions leading to unpredictability—an inclination that reminds one of Jean Paul's technique of telling a story—Schubert here weaves a net of motivic relationships which are partly open and partly latent (and which convey to a hearer, even when he does not perceive them consciously,a feeling of musical cohesion). The procedure varies. Measures 40-42, with which the second subject begins, are diastematically but not rhythmically derived from the continuation of the first theme (mm.14-15). Conversely, measures 86-87, the beginning of the closing section, offer a rhythmic but not diastematic reminiscence of measures 4-5 of the first theme.

Although one recognizes the effort to achieve firm cohesion and thematic-motivic density, Schubert seems at the same time to have yielded to the drive toward epic expansion—his original musical impulse. The transitions between first and second themes (mm. 21-39) and between second and closing themes (mm. 68-85) are long and leisurely spun out. The second of these connective passages, which has no modulatory function, has the character of an episode (the virtuoso element and the placement within the form remind one of the "playful episode" in piano concertos of the nineteenth century). The result of the double tendencies—toward cohesion, on one hand, and toward expansion, on the other—is a particular variation technique, problematic in a sonata movement. The transitions referred to are nothing other than variations or variants of the first and second themes. It would be an error to speak of sections that "develop" and thereby to blur terminologically the factual difference from Beethoven's technique of form. Variation technique, which means both cohesion and expansion, cancels the meaning that cohesion had for Beethoven and expansion for Schubert in his earlier sonatas: it produces the effect neither of concentration nor of thematic-melodic abundance. The tendencies which Schubert tried to weld together neutralize each other instead of reaching a successful compromise. The result is a combination of thematic sparseness and a trend toward long spun-out stretches, which Schumann rightly felt to be an aesthetic shortcoming.

The finale of the C-minor sonata, of more than seven hundred measures, is built on the simplest imaginable formal design so that the movement, notwithstanding its excessive extension, does not dissolve beyond comprehension:

Sections	A^1	B^1	C	A^2	B^2	A^3
Measures	1-112	113-242	243-428	429-498	499-660	661-717

The simplicity and solidity of the ground plan form the counterpart to the epic expansion.

With all simplicity of the design—shown by letter symbols, often a forced treatment doing aesthetic violence to a form but here quite adequate—the movement hardly fits into the system of musical forms as outlined in the early nineteenth century by Adolf Bernhard Marx. Reduction to sonata form or rondo form is possible but precarious inasmuch as a decision in favor of either of these two forms is difficult. Moreover, there is no telling whether renunciation of a decision and hence acceptance of formal "ambiguity" does justice to a movement whose formal outline favors a tendency toward simplicity rather than complexity. A critical place, either betraying a flaw or making a formal point, is the beginning of section C or the transition from B^1 to C. A hearer proceeding from the typical norm of a sonata finale expects either (according to the model of sonata form) a development section or (according to the layout of a rondo) a return of the ritornello A. The presentation by Schubert of a third theme must be confusing. The impression of a crumbling form and decline into a potpourri is prevented or delayed solely because a potpourri—a mere chain of themes—seems out of the question in a sonata finale. One looks spontaneously for a reason and justification to make the apparent deficiency of form acceptable as deception and misunderstanding. The placement and function of the movement within a larger organism of which the formal standard is prescribed by tradition forces the hearer to "strain the concept" in regard to formal aesthetics.

The explanation that the return of the ritornello *A* between *B* and *C* was omitted because one further repetition of the long drawn-out theme would have been intolerable, the hypothesis, in short, that the form is to be understood as an amputated rondo, is apparently persuasive because its simplicity fits that of the formal design; but it is insufficient. If one hears section *C* analytically— supported by the "prejudice" grounded in the tradition of the genre that a potpourri-like alternation could not possibly have been Schubert's formal thought—one finds that it tends toward the principle of development in sonata form. It consists of an exposition (mm. 243-308) and a development (mm. 309-428) in which three models, all of them split off from theme *C*, are treated in sequences. But one can also recognize in theme *C* the outline of a variant in the major mode of *A* (m. 67), although rendered indistinct through augmentation. The tone sequel $f\sharp$-$d\sharp$-$c\sharp$-$(a\sharp)$-b-$f\sharp$ appears as transposition of g-e-d-c-g. But if section *C* is nothing else but a transformation and representation of *A*, then the movement must be formally classified as a sonata-rondo—a rondo of which the first couplet returns in a recapitulation and is tonally treated as second subject, and of which the second couplet acts as a development.

In order not to appear as a mere design and shell spread over single events, a musical form ought indeed to be founded on the character and structure of the themes. Rondo themes and sonata-form themes differ to a degree which does not permit their interchange. Hence a reconciliation as required by the sonata-rondo is difficult.

The themes in the finale of the C-minor sonata are primarily, in their melodic statement, characteristic rondo themes. They present themselves as closed phrases, which indeed demand repetition; and repetition of parts is constitutive for a formation by groups like the rondo. The spun-out continuations of the themes (m. 25 and m. 145), however, tend toward formation by development: parts splitting off from the themes are treated in sequences by themselves or inserted in models of development.

The dual character of the thematic groups, the juxtaposition of features from different form traditions, is not a sign of uncertainty, which would be an aesthetic deficiency, but rather fulfills a function: in the structure of the individual themes, the form of the whole—the interlocking of sonata form and rondo—is prepared and established. The finale is not an amputated rondo tending toward a potpourri but a special case of sonata-rondo, aesthetically motivated down to the smallest detail.

Liszt: *Mazeppa*

Henri Stendhal defined classicism and romanticism as periods not of style but of aesthetic judgment of styles: classicism of today is romanticism of the past, and romanticism of the present is classicism of the future. The historic-philosophic hypothesis underlying Stendhal's terminology, however, has led to disappointment. The expectation has not been fulfilled that the romanticism of the nineteenth century, particularly the most advanced one which felt itself drawn toward program music, would be elevated to the status of classicism. Program music, the "new music" of the nineteenth century, has not become established in the twentieth century but antiquated.

Yet Stendhal's historic-philosophic thought is not just an empty speculation. According to popular notions of the nineteenth century, classicism—crudely labeled—inclines toward formalism whereas romanticism inclines toward an aesthetics of content. Hence the metamorphosis of romanticism to classicism means nothing else but that the content of musical works gradually pales and that their form or structure emerges all the more clearly and conspicuously. Although the aesthetics of program music is today regarded with contempt, Liszt's works, as one knows, are being eagerly investigated, particularly by musical "structuralists." The return to Liszt, which has become almost fashionable in the last decade and a half, indicates only a discovery of unorthodox techniques of composition, not a renaissance of the works as

aesthetic creations. Notwithstanding their admiring technical
interest in the methods, the critics view the results with aesthetic
mistrust.

   To avoid confusion, one must also distinguish between structure and form. To praise latent structures in Liszt's works as
discoveries in the technique of composition has become almost
commonplace among music historians, but criticism of form that
goes beyond mere cataloguing has barely begun. It would have to
assert itself in the precarious middle ground between analytic
interest and aesthetic indifference.

   In the nineteenth century, form theory of the musical
aesthetics of contents was dichotomous. Either one followed the
conviction that musical form, being secondary, could and even
should be schematic; it is no accident that the sonatas of the
romantics Weber and Chopin are formally more conventional than
those of the classic Beethoven. Or one accepted the opposite
postulate that form, depending on ever-changing content, had to be
individual and unique to each work. Content aesthetics can thus be
reconciled equally with formal schematism and with emancipation
from a schema, equally with tolerant justification and with rejection
of convention. The dichotomy extends to the conception of single
works or to their interpretation. Thus, the main section of the
symphonic poem *Mazeppa*—without the introduction and the
triumphal martial conclusion—admits of several formal interpretations which yet leave open the question whether the ambiguity is to
be assessed as differentiation or uncertainty, as a sign of emancipation or formal decay.

   The groundplan of the main section is formed by a chain of
variations (a fact not clearly demonstrated by earlier analyses). The
theme (m. 36) is divided into four functionally differentiated parts
(8+8+8+9 measures): antecedent, continuation, cadential epilogue,
and appendix or transition. In Variation I (m. 69), the antecedent
becomes chromatic. More specifically, the modification of the chord
progression C-F-E-A of the theme to C-f-E♭-A♭ retains an
undecided middle position between a modulation (or transposition)
and a chromatic alteration also affecting the roots of the chords (the
kind of chromatic alteration not admitted by theory). Continuation
and epilogue are exchanged. The correlate of the functional shifting

of the parts is melodic modification: the epilogue is transformed into the consequent. Variation II (m. 122) appears as the necessary result of I. First, the chromatic alteration becomes extreme inasmuch as it already affects the beginning of the theme. The tone progression *d-c-bb-a-e-g-f-a-d* becomes chromatically masked or estranged as *db-c-bb-a-gb-a-c-bb* (that is, D minor and B-flat minor). Second, the epilogue is again transformed into the consequent. The third Variation (m. 184) is at first a transposition of the second Variation from B-flat minor to B minor. Simultaneously, however, B minor appears as further chromatization of the D-minor theme—an "alternate chroma," as it were, of B-flat minor (the steps altered in B-flat minor remain intact in B minor, and vice versa). The end of the Variation (m. 216) is formed by an onset of a development of fragments from the antecedent. Variation IV (m. 232) is an apotheosis of the theme; Variation V (m. 263), a restoration of the original shape, a recapitulation. The sixth and last Variation (m. 317), like the first one, is a chromatic variant of the theme. The relation of Variations VI to II—analogously to the relation of Variations II to III—follows the principle of the "alternate chroma": the chord progression A-d-C-F-E-A of the theme is chromatized in Variation I to A-d-C-f-Eb-Ab, but in Variation VI to A-D-C♯-f♯-E-A.

The appearance of the variations as a cycle, a closed circle and not just a row or chain, is founded upon the combination with other complementary principles of form. Theme and Variation I unmistakably form a main section; Variations II to IV, a middle section; and V and VI, a recapitulation. The simple design of a "song form"—an unfortunately chosen but ineradicable term—does not suffice, however, to explain the transformation of the open to a closed form. The "song form" is modified by characteristics of sonata form. The elements pointing to sonata form were perceived all the more clearly in the nineteenth century because the derivation of the symphonic poem from overture and symphony readily suggested the presentation of a sonata form. The chromatic alteration of the theme in Variations I and VI offers a distant analogy to the changed tonality in the new key area of a sonata form. Paradoxically stated, the chromatization appears as modulation according to the norm of sonata form, on the condition of not modulating valid in a variation set. (The ambivalent harmonic technique might be the correlate of an unusual idea of form.) Other details of sonata form can be found in Variations III to V: the onset of a development (III), the emphatic triumph typical since Beethoven for the recapitulation as culmination and result of the development (IV), and finally the return of the theme in its original shape (V). Climax and recapitulation in *Mazeppa* are separate "times of the form," to use August Halm's language. The reason for the separation, which seems an aesthetic-formal flaw, and for the effect of the culmination of a forced "arranged" apotheosis and not of an achieved logical result probably lies in the brevity and immature condition of the development. Circumstantial treatment was obviously impossible in a variation set. The principles of form that encounter each other in *Mazeppa* do not mesh without contradiction. Ingenious solutions of difficulties—chromatization as modulation and as not-modulation—stand next to semi-failures— the splitting of the recapitulation.

It is no apologetic exaggeration to claim that the formal conception of *Mazeppa* is differentiated. One cannot deny, on the other hand, that the effect of the piece derives primarily from the relentlessly driving motion. According to the dogma of content aesthetics that Wagner shared with Liszt and explicated in his essay on Liszt's symphonic poems, musical form should remain inconspicuous. Form is not the end but a means toward the realization of the "poetic intent for feeling." Form is a formulation, in music as in language. A formulation is perfect when it is so completely adapted to the content it expresses as to remain unnoticeable as a formulation.

Inconspicuous to Wagner and Liszt was the individual musical form, dependent on changing content. Conspicuous to them was the conventional schema. The formalists they attacked appealed to norms. Yet the aesthetic-psychological facts are ambiguous. One could ask conversely whether the unusual form deviating from a norm does not become conspicuous by intruding as a form upon musical consciousness instead of remaining concealed as the mere intermediary of content.

One gets the impression that Liszt's aesthetics—through which Liszt's concepts of form suffer an injustice—enjoyed psychological validity in the nineteenth century. (Music psychology blind to history goes astray.) Adequate appreciation of the differentiated forms emanating from the interweaving of diverse principles in the symphonic poems has perhaps become possible only since the programmatic element has paled and sunk into irrelevance, and the classicistic formalism of the nineteenth century, which looked for the realization of a traditional type in a musical form, was superseded by the manneristic formalism of the twentieth century, which drives toward novelty and considers not the schematic but the unusual form as conspicuous. If this aesthetic-psychological hypothesis is correct, then Liszt's musical forms were not properly received in the nineteenth century: neither by the "new Germanic" followers who saw in form—as inconspicuous form—merely a function of the content, nor by the opponents who, being classicistic formalists, misconstrued as formless and rejected the unusual form conceptions of the symphonic poems.

Mahler: Second Symphony, finale

The symphonic cantata, as it was called in the nineteenth century, is one of the genres not established as a genre at all. Not that it might be a hybrid mixture—the aesthetic postulate of the "purity of genres" is of classicistic origin and lost significance in the nineteenth century (it was discarded as "ridiculous" by Friedrich Schlegel). Yet the symphonic cantata appears as the paradox of a genre full of exceptional works: from the finale of Beethoven's Ninth Symphony past Mendelssohn's *Lobgesang*, Berlioz's *Romeo et Juliette*, and Liszt's *Dante* and *Faust* symphonies to Mahler's symphonies. Special forms which stand next to each other as single, historically isolated, and not mutually conditioned mediators between symphony and cantata do not create a genre inasmuch as this concept needs a tradition from which the single works arise and gain substance even when resisting the norms of the genre.

The concept of symphonic cantata implies, on the other hand, a form problem with always the same outline. It consists, negatively formulated, in the difficulty of not only avoiding a mere juxtaposition of symphony and cantata, of heterogeneous self-sufficient parts, but also of circumventing the disproportion when either the cantata shrivels to an appendix of the symphony (as in Liszt's *Faust*) or the symphony to a prelude of the cantata.

It lies in the nature of the case or in the European musical tradition that the vocal part always appears as the goal and end of the instrumental part, never the other way around—perhaps because the accumulation of means produces an end effect or because the more definite linguistic expression is felt to be a consequence of the less definite musical expression which it, as it were, redeems. The problem of form which Mahler had to solve in the finale of the Second Symphony (the "Resurrection" symphony) can be described as the paradoxical task of mediating between symphony and cantata in such a way that the symphonic part is self-sufficient and yet preserves the character of an introduction. (The restriction of this analysis to the problem of form may seem a reduction to an unessential or secondary feature; but it is justified insofar as nobody, not even his opponents, doubts the expressive and rhetorical force of Mahler's symphonies.)

The instrumental part of the finale has the overall character of an introduction, which could be described as a particular case of the typical symphonic drive toward a goal. The beginning, sixty measures over a single organ point which fastens the music to one spot, acts as introduction to the introduction. It is put together of a dissonant tonal field, vague outlines and tentative onsets of the finale themes interlocked with reminiscences of the first movement, and finally a chain of roving chords which do not relate tonally one to another and thus share with the standing sounds the mark of not being developmental.

The first phrase of the main theme (4 mm. after no. 4) is nothing but a return to the first movement (17 mm. after no. 16), so that the finale appears as the consequence and summation of earlier parts of the composition. The second phrase (no. 5), anticipating the beginning of the cantata, "Auferstehn," forms the central theme of the finale. (It, too, is a reminiscence of the first movement but only partially—3 mm. after no. 5 in the finale equals 7 mm. after no. 17 in the first movement—and with a rhythmic variant that obscures the connection.) The second subject (no. 7), similarly an anticipation of a cantata melody, offers an extreme contrast to the main theme. After the second subject, the first is repeated (no. 10-14), creating a closed ternary form instead of exposing the thematic dualism in an open binary form which would demand an immediate unfolding and development. Both the first and second themes, with all their sharp divergence, are "rhetorical" themes. Their vocal quality—chorale and also dramatic-expressive gesture—cannot be missed. The speech character of the motives forms the exact correlate of the formal double function fulfilled by the instrumental part. On one hand, we almost feel able to anticipate the words, of which the themes are the expression, so that the later vocal version appears prefigured. On the other hand, the themes can exist as instrumental formations by themselves and serve as the foundation of a symphonic movement precisely because they are extremely expressive and eloquent, having completely absorbed the vocal into the instrumental element. (A less expressive instrumental recitative would act as a mere shadow and reflex of vocalism.)

The vocal part of the finale, the cantata, fulfills the formal function of a recapitulation but relates to the instrumental exposition as a finished execution to the sketch. Themes which in the exposition were fragmentary and almost tentative onsets (6 mm. after no. 2; 3 mm. after no. 11) are at the end of the movement broadly elaborated and developed so that the original primary themes, while returning unabridged, seem repressed and reduced in importance. The displacement of emphasis is not an accident but the result of formal calculation. One of the reasons behind Mahler's solution of the form problem of the symphonic cantata is that the themes or motives predominating in the exposition stand in the shadow in the recapitulation and the other way around. (Characteristic in this respect, as already mentioned, is the placement in the exposition of the "Auferstehn" melody in the consequent—in the secondary section—of the main theme.) The cantata is, on the one hand, the recapitulation of the symphonic exposition; the transition to vocalism seems almost the necessary consequence of the emphasis placed since Beethoven on a recapitulation as the goal and result of the development. By regroupings, on the other hand, in the hierarchy of themes whereby originally secondary motives become prominent and primary motives pale, the cantata preserves its independence as a vocal piece distinguished from the instrumental.

An unambiguous formal determination of the middle section (no. 14) is difficult and nearly impossible. The programmatic meaning of a march with traits of a dance of death is so drastic as to repress any reflection on formal functions. The employment of a march for the finale of a symphony is not unusual and does not need to be justified. The emphatically irresistible drive, moreover, suggests a goal to be reached so that the march fulfills the aesthetic postulate of attributing to the instrumental part of a symphonic cantata the overall character of an introduction. Decisive in criticism of form, however, is whether the march is to be understood as a development section or not. Many features point toward a development. Themes from the exposition (and from the first movement) are drawn into the march which finally, in analogy to the first movement (no. 18), reaches a climax signifying not a conclusion but rather a collapse (no. 20). There is no dearth of hidden and complex motivic relationships. The march theme (11 mm. after no. 15), partly a reminiscence of the *Dies irae,* also derives from paraphrasing a motive (no. 15) calling to mind the main theme (4 mm. after no. 4) in regard to rhythm and diastematic outline. Yet the statement that the middle section is a development is not only true but also false. It is true because themes from the exposition are taken up and involved in an urgent drive typical of a development since Beethoven. It is also false because the themes are not subjected to thematic-motivic elaboration but are only quoted and dragged along in the dance of death projected by the music.

If one does not view the march as a development, then the formal importance of the vocal part is certainly diminished. In the ABA form, which one would then have to assume, the return of the beginning sounds less convincingly and emphatically like a recapitulation than in a situation in which the recapitulation emerges as the goal and result of the development. The aesthetic argument can be complemented by a historic-psychological one. The traditions of genre and form, from which a work springs, belong to its substance, to the issue itself and not merely to the conditions of its origin. In the finale of a symphony, the traits of sonata form, even when weakly delineated, stand out conspicuously because sonata form is the schema expected by the hearer. (Therefore one may establish in analysis the rule that a movement is to be interpreted, within sensible limits, as a variant of the form characteristic of the genre, and not as exemplifying another schema unusual for the genre.

Schönberg: Third String Quartet, opus 30

One of the main principles of Schönberg's aesthetics—masked as instruction in a craft—derives from the concept of analogy, according to which all parts of a composition have to be equally developed to avoid fracture. The composers and theoreticians of serial music, however, who gathered in 1951 around the watchword "Schönberg est mort," turned the analogy principle against Schönberg himself. They reproached him for the inconsistency and aesthetic-technical flaw of having restricted his serial technique to pitch progressions or the diastematic order of tone qualities to the exclusion of rhythm and dynamics. (The polemics were a kind of apology for their own serial procedure which solved the contradiction they believed to have found in Schönberg's music.) Atonal diastematics, they claimed, had been forced together by Schönberg with "tonal" rhythms (that is, rhythms created in connection with tonal harmony), so that the various components of a work, contrary to the analogy postulate, appear unequally developed and representative of diverse historical grades.

Schönberg's "tonal" traditional rhythm (so continued the criticism) offers in works like the Third and Fourth String Quartets the proposition of restoring the "tonal" sonata form under atonal conditions, a restoration both violent and illusory. The attempt to reconstruct the sonata form, out of a historically delayed desire for the "large form," must fail, for its substance—tonality—has crumbled and its time has passed. And the mark of historic or philosophic fruitlessness is aesthetic failure.

The first movement of the Third String Quartet, written in 1927, clearly follows sonata form without tonal support or justification. The disposition is almost overly explicit, as if to drown out the loss of the tonal foundation. One does not deal, however, with a merely decorative form without substance and carelessly pulled over the musical events. The argument that sonata form is primarily based on tonality—on the contrast between tonic and dominant and on the difference between tonally closed and modulating sections—equates the origin of the type with its essence and neglects the historic development the form experienced in the nineteenth century. In the chamber music of Brahms, the structural organization of the sonata form derives less from the arrangement of keys, difficult to perceive, than from the contrast of themes, which generates the thematic-motivic elaboration. Schönberg's procedure of committing the formal articulation exclusively to the thematic structure while excluding tonality is indeed an extreme, one-sided manifestation of the sonata-form principle but not its abolition or depletion. Schönberg's traditionalism is not so naive as the historian-philosophers among his detractors think. (The thesis that the median compromise between harmonic-tonal and thematic-motivic foundation provides the ideal type of sonata form rests on a dogmatic preference for classicism: the early developmental stage of the form, in which tonal order is decisive, would appear as a rudimentary onset; the late stage, in which thematic elaboration predominates, as decay.)

Weak and analytically ill-founded is also the claim that, after the collapse of tonality, the themes of sonata-form movements consist of bare rhythms, only secondarily "outfitted" with pitches by the tone rows. In such a case, the themes fall apart into a rhythmic scaffolding and a diastematic filler and become contradictory and split in two like the overall form built upon them. This prejudice started through an exaggerated interpretation of an otherwise valid observation. The first and second subjects (mm. 5 and 62) appear in the recapitulation in reverse order (the first subject in m. 235, the second in m. 174) but also in diastematic inversion with unchanged rhythm, so that one might be tempted to interpret the identical rhythm as the substance, and the variable pitch progression as an accidental property, of the themes. The themes, moreover, seem to flow into each other. The first theme is based primarily on the main form and retrograde inversion of the row; the second theme, on the inversion and retrograde form. The diastematic inversion in the recapitulation thus indicates an exchange of the row forms between first and second subjects (but not an exchange of the actual tone progressions, for the themes are composed of fragments of the rows of which the remaining tones become accompaniment): main form and retrograde inversion change into inversion and retrograde form; inversion and retrograde form change into main form and retrograde inversion.

Yet the thesis that rhythm and diastematics in the Third String Quartet are torn apart is not valid. The real thematic substance, whose development makes the movement intelligible to the hearer, are not the rhythms and tone progressions of the first and second subjects as a whole but the very smallest elements: firmly designed and ever recurring rhythmic figures as well as definite intervals and groups of intervals. The first subject is based on two rhythmic *klang* feet, as Johann Mattheson would say, on the spondee (— —) and the creticus (— ◡ —); the second subject, on the spondee and the iamb (◡ —). The intervallic inventory of the themes is restricted to the semitone, minor third, fourth, and tritone as well as their inversions. Wholetone and major third are absent. The reduction and apparent impoverishment, however, are the prerequisite or reverse side of a wealth of relationships which are thoroughly audible. The themes are nothing else but ever new groupings of the same rhythms and intervals. Through the identity within the change, and the variability within the return, rhythms and intervals become interwoven: the technique of variants creates interrelations between the "parameters." In no case does the Third Quartet deserve the reproach that Schönberg used it to dissolve the traditional connection between pitch progression and rhythm without replacing it by a serial connection, or that he filled in thematic rhythms with arbitrarily exchangeable, accidental, and almost irrelevant forms of the row.

The basic principle of sonata form restored by dodecaphony— after the decay of key disposition—is the development technique, the thematic elaboration, which in the Third String Quartet, however, is open to the criticism of being tautological. Dodecaphony, the web of inversions, transpositions, and fragmentations of the row—so the criticism goes—is itself nothing but an extreme consequence and historically last step of thematic elaboration which in twelve-tone compositions, in which each note is deduced from the row, extends across the whole movement instead of restricting itself to the developing part of the exposition and to the development section itself. Thematic elaboration, as Theodor W. Adorno expressed it, is "pushed back into the material"; because the "deformation" of the material generally consists of thematic elaboration at every instance, thematic elaboration as a specific technique of the composition becomes a superfluous duplication. Sonata form, the criticism continues, is without substance, because the only substance left to it after the dissolution of tonality, namely, thematic elaboration, is "annulled" by serial technique proper—before the act of composing—and can thus not be constitutive for a particular form.

The construct that dodecaphony originated with thematic elaboration and represents its historic goal and end ignores the trivial fact that a tone progression without rhythm is not a theme but only an abstract ingredient of a theme. Hence the equation of dodecaphonic structure with thematic elaboration appears as a doubtful exaggeration. With good reason, Rudolf Réti—whose method clearly bears the stamp of experience with dodecaphony even when he analyzes Beethoven sonatas—distinguishes between open motivic relations, which are always rhythmic-melodic relations, and latent diastematic connections, which reveal themselves only by abstraction from rhythm (an abstraction toward which theoreticians like August Halm and Heinrich Schenker incline who occupy estranged or inimical positions against dodecaphony). If Réti's analyses are correct, the traces of a prehistory of dodecaphony would have to be sought in the latent diastematic combinations (which are independent of the difference between the thematic and nonthematic sections of a movement). Judging these analyses, however, presupposes difficult aesthetic and historic-philosophic decisions. Does a Beethoven analysis of which the fundamental principle—separation of diastematics and rhythm—was foreign to musical feeling around 1800 still make sense when one succeeds without force in decoding in the musical text a structure which is not only consistent in itself but also links essential parts of the work to each other? Can a method nourished by experiences with new music, without which it would not be thinkable, lead to discoveries in older music or just to fictions? Is the essence of compositions, rather than standing invariably fixed *sub specie aeternitatis,* subject to development so that the history of interpretations could be understood as the expression of a history of the compositions themselves? Is it possible to speak of historic variability of works without sacrificing their identity? There is no end to the reflections evoked by the attempt to establish relationships between analysis, aesthetics, history, and philosophy of history.